12th Web as Corpus Workshop (ACL SIGWAC 2020)

Marseille, France
11 – 16 May 2020

Editors:

Adrien Barbaresi
Felix Bildhauer
Roland Schafer
Egon Stemle

ISBN: 978-1-7138-1251-7

Printed from e-media with permission by:

Curran Associates, Inc.
57 Morehouse Lane
Red Hook, NY 12571

CURRAN ASSOCIATES INC. proceedings.com

Some format issues inherent in the e-media version may also appear in this print version.

Association for Computational Linguistics
209 N. Eighth Street
Stroudsburg, Pennsylvania 18360

Phone: 1-570-476-8006
Fax: 1-570-476-0860

acl@aclweb.org

Additional copies of this publication are available from:

Curran Associates, Inc.
57 Morehouse Lane
Red Hook, NY 12571 USA
Phone: 845-758-0400
Fax: 845-758-2633
Email: curran@proceedings.com
Web: www.proceedings.com

LREC 2020 Workshop
Language Resources and Evaluation Conference
11–16 May 2020

The 12th Web as Corpus Workshop
(ACL SIGWAC)

PROCEEDINGS

Editors:
Adrien Barbaresi, Felix Bildhauer, Roland Schäfer and Egon Stemle

Proceedings of the LREC 2020 12th Web as Corpus Workshop (ACL SIGWAC)

Edited by: Adrien Barbaresi, Felix Bildhauer, Roland Schäfer and Egon Stemle

Organizers:

Adrien Barbaresi, BBAW Berlin, DE
Felix Bildhauer, IDS Mannheim & Humboldt-Universität zu Berlin, DE
Roland Schäfer, Humboldt-Universität zu Berlin, DE
Egon Stemle, Eurac Research, IT

Program Committee:

Piotr Banski, IDS Mannheim, DE
Silvia Bernardini, University of Bologna, IT
Stefan Evert, University of Erlangen, DE
Miloš Jakubíček, SketchEngine, UK
Simon Krek, Jožef Stefan Institute, SI
Nikola Ljubešić, Jožef Stefan Institute, SI
Elizabeth Pankratz, University of Potsdam, DE
Steffen Remus, University of Hamburg, DE
Serge Sharoff, University of Leeds, UK
Wajdi Zaghouani, Hamad Bin Khalifa University, QA

Felix Bildhauer's and Roland Schäfer's work was partially funded by the Deutsche Forschungsgegemeinschaft (German Research Foundadtion) – SFB 1412 Register – 416591334

Introduction

For almost fifteen years, the ACL SIGWAC, and most notably the Web as Corpus (WAC) workshops, have served as a platform for researchers interested in the compilation, processing and use of web-derived corpora as well as computer-mediated communication. Past workshops were co-located with major conferences on corpus linguistics and computational linguistics (such as ACL, EACL, Corpus Linguistics, LREC, NAACL, WWW).

In corpus linguistics and theoretical linguistics, the World Wide Web has become increasingly popular as a source of linguistic evidence, especially in the face of data sparseness or the lack of variation in traditional corpora of written language. In lexicography, web data have become a major and well-established resource with dedicated research data and specialised tools. In other areas of theoretical linguistics, the adoption rate of web corpora has been slower but steady. Furthermore, some completely new areas of linguistic research dealing exclusively with web (or similar) data have emerged, such as the construction and utilisation of corpora based on short messages. Another example is the (manual or automatic) classification of web texts by genre, register, or – more generally speaking – "text type", as well as topic area. In computational linguistics, web corpora have become an established source of data for the creation of language models, word embeddings, and all types of machine learning.

The 12th Web as Corpus workshop (WAC-XII) looks at the past, present, and future of web corpora given the fact that large web corpora are nowadays provided mostly by a few major initiatives and companies, and the diversity of the early years appears to have faded slightly. Also, we acknowledge the fact that alternative sources of data (such as data from Twitter and similar platforms) have emerged, some of them only available to large companies and their affiliates, such as linguistic data from social media and other forms of the deep web. At the same time, gathering interesting and relevant web data (web crawling) is becoming an ever more intricate task as the nature of the data offered on the web changes (for example the death of forums in favour of more closed platforms).

This year's edition will not lead to a half-day workshop at the LREC 2020 conference as expected. The full proceedings remain, of which the present volume is a part.

We received 13 submissions in total, the proceedings comprise 8 articles.

We would like to thank the reviewers for their help and wish to see you at the next edition under better circumstances.

The organizers:

Adrien Barbaresi
Felix Bildhauer
Roland Schäfer
Egon Stemle

Table of Contents

Proceedings of the 12th Web as Corpus Workshop, pages 1–4
Language Resources and Evaluation Conference (LREC 2020), Marseille, 11–16 May 2020

Current Challenges in Web Corpus Building

Miloš Jakubíček, Vojtěch Kovář, Pavel Rychlý, Vít Suchomel
Lexical Computing & Masaryk University

Abstract

In this paper we discuss some of the current challenges in web corpus building that we faced in the recent years when expanding the corpora in Sketch Engine. The purpose of the paper is to provide an overview and raise discussion on possible solutions, rather than bringing ready solutions to the readers. For every issue we try to assess its severity and briefly discuss possible mitigation options.

1. Introduction

Web corpus building has been the major way of obtaining large text collections for almost two decades now (see (Kilgarriff and Grefenstette, 2003) for a starting point and (Schäfer and Bildhauer, 2013) for a current overview) and there have been many web corpora built isolated (using methods such as WebBootCat (Baroni et al.,)) or as part of a bigger corpus family such as (Jakubíček et al., 2013), (Benko, 2014) or (Biemann et al., 2007).

Web corpora have been used as the primary source of linguistic evidence for many purposes. Besides linguistic research itself, the main areas of application included development and evaluation of natural language processing tools and methods, computer lexicography or practical analysis of large texts for varying tasks like trends or topics monitoring.

Building corpora from web has become popular for all the advantages it brings: small building costs, high speed of building and prospects on getting a very large dataset that would perform well in Zipfian distribution were reasons that are still very relevant, perhaps even more than before as NLP becomes more widespread and used in projects on a daily basis and many NLP methods (such as word embeddings) rely on large text corpora.

Sadly, most of the disadvantages of using web corpora have not been overcome in the 20 years: web corpora still provide only a very limited set of metadata, it is still difficult to clean the web content automatically and on the legal front there has not been any significant progress that would clarify the legal status of the datasets[1].

In this paper we are not going to discuss the advantages and disadvantages of web corpus building but take a very practical look at the biggest obstacles for web corpus building as of 2020. The starting point for all reasoning is that one aims at building a corpus from web which should be as big as possible and as clean as possible, where by clean we merely restrict ourselves to technical cleaning: yielding well-formed and well-encoded documents containing human-produced natural language texts, ideally (but not necessarily) split into paragraphs or sentences.

The issues that we mention are basically those that we have faced in the recent years when building corpora for the TenTen corpus family programme.(Jakubíček et al., 2013)

[1] In the European Union. In the US, the case law on related projects like Google Books (`https://en.wikipedia.org/wiki/Authors_Guild,_Inc._v._Google,_Inc.`) paved the way for more relaxed web corpus usage.

2. Current Issues

2.1. Machine Translation

2.1.1. The problem

Machine translation is ubiquitous on the web. Surprisingly, it is rather low-resourced language webs affected the most by machine translation, where the quality of machine translation is often very poor, but the market size simply does not make the case for human translation. Website owners are therefore confronted with a rather simple choice: either no content for that particular low-resourced language, or (poor, but) machine translated. Where reputation does not play a big role (and that means: hobbyists, fans, cheap sales websites, blogs platforms etc.), the choice is frequently to use machine translation, whatever its quality would be.

2.1.2. Mitigation strategies

Detecting machine translated content automatically is very difficult and there are no language-independent methods with reasonable precision-recall trade offs. Recall that this is in the first place a problem for low-resourced languages, which typically suffer from limited online content anyway. Thus applying any high-recall/low-precision strategies likely harms the size of the resulting dataset significantly and the most efficient way lies in using semi-automated methods: typically this involves hiring a native speaker for several days, checking the corpus wordlist and most represented web domains to discover "nests" of machine translated content and remove the whole domains. The general rule of thumb is: if a website offers many language versions, it is likely that most or all are machine translated. If there is an Esperanto version, it is always machine translated. In one of the most recent crawls of Estonian, which was carried out at the end of 2019 to create Estonian National Corpus 2019 (Kallas et al., 2015) in collaboration with the Institute for Estonian Language, we have generated a list of 600 most represented web domains which were manually inspected and 110 sites were removed from the corpus since their content was computer generated.

Another observation was made when cleaning a Lao Web corpus from 2019. 761 of 991 (77 %) domains with URI paths beginning with "/lo/" were identified as "bad language" by a Lao native speaker[2] based on samples of texts from particular domains. Since many of these bad language samples looked like machine translated, our hypothesis that

[2] Native speakers were asked to choose from three options: "good", "bad" or "I can't tell"

URI path can indicate machine translated content was confirmed. Together with a manual inspection of most represented domains in the corpus, approximately 9 % of tokens in the corpus were removed.

2.1.3. Severity

The severity of this issue is very high. The whole point about building corpora is to provide authentic evidence of language use and anything that hampers this idea represents a serious problem.

2.2. Spam

2.2.1. The problem

Spam represents a similar issue to the machine-generated content in terms that it also brings unnatural and thus unwanted content into the corpus. While it may not necessarily be automatically generated, it frequently is and spammers have been improving the text generation algorithms (including by means of applying NLP methods) during their long battle with search engines over the past years. There are, however, notable differences from the machine-translated content that have huge impact on how this should be dealt with. While machine translation is used permanently, intentionally (by website owners) and legally, spam typically occurs on someone's website as its temporary, illegal and random misuse. Such hacked websites are then used a honeypot to bring the user to some (less temporary, but also not very permanent) target site.

The illegality is also related to the topic of spamming: it tends to cover areas that are (in a particular country) prohibited or massively regulated, such as drugs, pharmacy, lottery, guns, loans and mortgages or prostitution. The topic heavily depends on the country and its regulations.

The temporal aspects of spam fighting may be crucial to fight it successfully. In our experience it was almost never possible to access a spam site several weeks after it has been crawled, because it was already cleaned and either shut down or previous content was restored. It is also likely the reason why search engines seem to fight spam rather well by analyzing its dynamic and temporary properties, but for web crawling by means of taking a static snapshot of a web, it is still a serious issue. During the past five years we have been regularly discovering spam sites where it took several minutes for a trained NLP engineers to conclude that this is a spam site. The spam site was mimicking a regular institutional website (such as of an U.S. university) including all its typical parts (courses, enrollment etc.), but starting with level 3 or 4 of nested links on the website, spam content was found which was completely unrelated to the institution. Notably, the institution was completely made up, so this was not a hacked institutional website, but a hacked domain with completely invented content.

2.2.2. Mitigation strategies

Automatic mitigation strategies may focus on the temporal aspects of spamming and involve:

- starting the crawl from a set of trustworthy seed domains obtained from web directories such as curlie.org, formerly dmoz.org, lists of newspapers (e.g. onlinenewspapers.com) which are less likely to get hacked
- measuring domain distance from seed domains and not deviating too deep from the seed domains
- using hostname heuristics (long hostnames consisting of multiple words are likely to be computer generated and containing spam)

Manual strategies are similar to the machine translation but thanks to the fact that spam is, unlike machine translated content, topical, one can use more analytic approaches than just looking up most frequent domains. Inspecting the usual suspects (like *viagra*, *loan*, *lottery*, ...) by means of collocations (in our case, word sketches) or other analytical tools can quickly reveal lot of spam content.

A complete solution to this problem would basically involve the same efforts that search engines put into this which is typically not feasible for a small company or NLP department. Out of all the aspects of spam, the temporality makes it most vulnerable: having most of the web indexed and permanently checking updates allows the crawler to temporarily suspend domains that suddenly completely or significantly change the content and this strategy could largely prevent getting spam into corpora without introducing any biases.

2.2.3. Severity

This is a very severe issue for the same reason like the ones given for machine translated texts.

2.3. Closed Content

2.3.1. The problem

Web crawling began as soon as Internet was sufficiently populated with texts. At that time, Internet consisted mostly of (plain) texts and as it became widespread in the developed world, everybody – institutions, companies, shops – went online, providing lots of natural language usage. Unfortunately, in many less developed countries where Internet became widespread later, going online meant creating a social network profile. As result, in these countries the Internet outside of social networks is simply much smaller and many companies and institutions have merely a Facebook page. Thus, while the Internet is now easily accessible, widespread and those countries are heavily populated, one only gets a fraction by crawling publicly accessible websites compared to similarly sized (in terms of native speakers) developed countries e.g. in Europe.

An example is e.g. Laos, a country with over 7 million citizens out of which over 25 % are online [3] where after extensive crawling for about half a year we were only able to obtain (after cleaning) a corpus of about 100 million words (whereas, in a country like Slovenia with 2 million citizens out of which almost 80 % are online, one can crawl a billion-word-sized corpus with no extra efforts).

We have also experienced more multimedia usage in these countries over textual content. But whether this is an unrelated issue or not would require more investigation.

[3]Data taken from `https://en.wikipedia.org/wiki/List_of_countries_by_number_of_Internet_users`.

2.3.2. Mitigation strategies

None. This paragraph might be a simple as that. Accessing social network content programmatically for the purposes of web crawling is typically not only illegal, but also technically very limited or impossible. Also, after more and more data privacy scandals around many social networks, their policies for data access and sharing have been tightened a lot and there are no prospects of this changing anytime soon. When people switch from open internet to closed platforms, it is over for linguistic web crawling.

2.3.3. Severity

This is a non-issue for "old" internet countries, big issue for "new" internet countries and generally a threat for the future if more and more online content is being shifted from open internet into closed (social media-like) platforms.

2.4. Dynamic Content

2.4.1. The problem

Modern websites rely more and more on dynamic content that is rendered in the client browser. While this brings better user experience and new functionalities, it also represents quite a technical challenge when crawling the texts from such websites. If yielding the texts requires rendering the content using a browser engine, it slows down the processing of a single website by several orders of magnitude.

2.4.2. Mitigation strategies

The only general solution really is to run a browser in headless mode and pass each found website to it, render its content as HTML and process it as usual. Some websites offer an HTML-only version to mobile browsers but it is not clear whether this could be applied generally (many other websites may still not be very mobile friendly).

2.4.3. Severity

The severity of this issue is so far rather low because websites still tend to provide textual fallback (e.g. for old mobile phones). As soon as they stop doing so, crawling will need to involve website rendering.

2.5. Paid Content

2.5.1. The problem

Early internet witnessed free news which, when the Internet population started to rise, were accompanied by ads. It is now clear that this was only a transition model from printed to online news and the revenues from online advertising (severely hindered by many users intentionally using tools for blocking adverts) are not sufficient to replace the fallen revenues on printed media subscriptions. Increasingly more media publishers therefore investigate new business models that incorporate online subscriptions (Fletcher and Nielsen, 2017) and a freemium model (a limited number of free articles per month, or limited set of articles, with other being paid) slowly becomes the new standard. Unfortunately the same news sources often represented valuable parts of the web corpus and if they become entirely missing, a whole genre of texts might become omitted.

2.5.2. Mitigation strategies

If at some point indeed most, or most quality, newspapers become completely unavailable without paying, web crawling such websites will either require paying (typically very modest) fee for a regular subscription or negotiating some access with the newspapers. The most problematic part is that this would require a per-website solution which significantly harms the current scalability of web crawling. Even if one manages to negotiate free access to the newspapers, it will still require developing customized solutions to incorporate data from that particular news.

2.5.3. Severity

Not very severe as long as reasonable amount of the newspaper text type remains freely accessible. But after that, this will represent an issue mainly for linguistic research focusing on this particular genre of texts.

3. Conclusion

In this paper we briefly discuss some issues of web crawling that we have stumbled upon most frequently in the recent years. The list is by no means complete and comprehensive and its whole purpose is to raise discussion at the workshop around the individual issues, possibly sharing further ideas on how to mitigate them.

Trying to predict the future of web crawling is tempting but of course hard. One may though imagine that the homogeneous Internet, as we know it now, slowly collapses into:

- content provided through some kind of web applications, possibly close or available only after payment
- the rest

The key question is how big the rest is going to be and whether it will be big enough and of sufficient quality to keep web crawling serving its current purpose. If not, it will require different approaches, which we may not even call crawling then.

4. Acknowledgements

This project has received funding from the European Union's Horizon 2020 research and innovation programme under grant agreement No 731015. This work has been partly supported by the Ministry of Education of CR within the LINDAT-CLARIAH-CZ project LM2018101 and by the Grant Agency of CR within the project 18-23891S.

5. Bibliographical References

Baroni, M., Kilgarriff, A., Pomikálek, J., Rychlý, P., et al.). Webbootcat: instant domain-specific corpora to support human translators.

Benko, V. (2014). Aranea: Yet another family of (comparable) web corpora. In *International Conference on Text, Speech, and Dialogue*, pages 247–256. Springer.

Biemann, C., Heyer, G., Quasthoff, U., and Richter, M. (2007). The leipzig corpora collection-monolingual corpora of standard size. *Proceedings of Corpus Linguistic*, 2007.

Fletcher, R. and Nielsen, R. K. (2017). Paying for online news. *Digital Journalism*, 5(9):1173–1191.

Jakubíček, M., Kilgarriff, A., Kovář, V., Rychlý, P., and Suchomel, V. (2013). The tenten corpus family. *Corpus Linguistics 2013*, page 125.

Kallas, J., Kilgarriff, A., Koppel, K., Kudritski, E., Langemets, M., Michelfeit, J., Tuulik, M., and Viks, Ü. (2015). Automatic generation of the estonian collocations dictionary database. In *Electronic lexicography in the 21st century: linking lexical data in the digital age. Proceedings of the eLex 2015 conference*, pages 11–13.

Kilgarriff, A. and Grefenstette, G. (2003). Introduction to the special issue on the web as corpus. *Computational linguistics*, 29(3):333–347.

Schäfer, R. and Bildhauer, F. (2013). Web corpus construction. *Synthesis Lectures on Human Language Technologies*, 6(4):1–145.

Proceedings of the 12th Web as Corpus Workshop, pages 5–13
Language Resources and Evaluation Conference (LREC 2020), Marseille, 11–16 May 2020

Out-of-the-Box and Into the Ditch? Multilingual Evaluation of Generic Text Extraction Tools

Adrien Barbaresi[1], Gaël Lejeune[2]
(1) Berlin-Brandenburg Academy of Sciences (2) Sorbonne University
Jägerstraße 22-23 10117 Berlin (Germany) / 1 rue Victor Cousin 75005 Paris (France)
barbaresi@bbaw.de / gael.lejeune@sorbonne-universite.fr

Abstract

This article examines extraction methods designed to retain the main text content of web pages and discusses how the extraction could be oriented and evaluated: can and should it be as generic as possible to ensure opportunistic corpus construction? The evaluation grounds on a comparative benchmark of open-source tools used on pages in five different languages (Chinese, English, Greek, Polish and Russian), it features several metrics to obtain more fine-grained differentiations. Our experiments highlight the diversity of web page layouts across languages or publishing countries. These discrepancies are reflected by diverging performances so that the right tool has to be chosen accordingly.

Keywords: Web corpus construction, Web Content Extraction, Boilerplate removal, Evaluation metrics, Cleaneval

1. Introduction

1.1. Web corpus construction

Large "offline" web corpora are now standard throughout disciplines among the research community. Corpus construction notably involves "crawling, downloading, 'cleaning' and de-duplicating the data, then linguistically annotating it and loading it into a corpus query tool." (Kilgarriff, 2007) Although text is ubiquitous on the Web, extracting information from web pages can prove to be difficult. They come in different shapes and sizes mostly because of the wide variety of platforms and content management systems, and not least depending on the context, for instance diverging goals followed during publication. This process involves a significant number of design decisions and turning points in data processing. Depending on the purpose of data collection, a substantial filtering and quality assessment can be crucial.

Recently, approaches using the CommonCrawl[1] have flourished as they allow for faster download and processing by skipping (or more precisely outsourcing) the crawling phase (Habernal et al., 2016; Schäfer, 2016). Barring the fact that finding one's "own" way through the Web can be preferable, it is clear that such data should not be used without some filtering. Beside the discovery of relevant websites, a major issue consist in selecting appropriate content after download and processing (Schäfer et al., 2013), which may not be straightforward due to unexpected or machine-generated flaws and biases. Some large-scale algorithms can be expected to smooth out irregularities. However, uses requiring a low margin of error and close reading approaches imply constant refinements in the constitution and processing of the dataset, for example in the context of an aggregated lexical information platform (Geyken et al., 2017).

The potential lack of metadata is worsened by a lack of information regarding the content whose adequacy, focus and quality are the object of a *post hoc* evaluation (Baroni et al., 2009). A major challenge lies in the ability to extract and pre-process web data to meet scientific expectations with respect to corpus quality (Barbaresi, 2015). Because of the vastly increasing variety of corpora, text types and use cases, it becomes more and more difficult to assess the usefulness and appropriateness of the gathered web texts for given research objectives. Potential answers can reside in methods such as focused web crawling for corpus construction (Schäfer et al., 2014) and in a degree of focus concerning the selection of sources (Barbaresi, 2016; Barbaresi, 2019).

Regardless of the chosen construction method, an essential operation consists in retaining the desired content while discarding the rest, a polyonymous goal referring to peculiar subtasks or to the whole, most notably web scraping, boilerplate removal, web page segmentation, web page cleaning, or content extraction (Lejeune and Zhu, 2018). The variety of contexts and text genres leads to important design decisions during the collection of texts: could and should the tooling be adapted to particular sources that are targeted (which often amounts to the development of web scraping tools e.g. for news outlets) or should the extraction be as generic as possible to provide opportunistic ways of gathering information? Due to a lack of time resources in academia and elsewhere, the tools are considered as field-tested without a thorough evaluation *in vitro*. This article hopefully makes a step towards the latter.

1.2. State of the art of content extraction

As the use of templates is pervasive on the Web (Bar-Yossef and Rajagopalan, 2002), common approaches to main content detection include heuristic rules, machine learning on labeled training data, and indirectly template-based approaches (for example by identifying duplicated content) (Rae et al., 2018). Although text-based (Kohlschütter and Nejdl, 2008) and visual segmentation algorithms (Cai et al., 2003) have been published on, content extraction mostly draws on Document Object Model (DOM) examination (Gupta et al., 2003). That means considering a given HTML document as a tree structure whose nodes represent parts of the document to be operated on.

[1] https://commoncrawl.org

Text, tag and/or link density have proven to be good heuristics in order to select or discard content nodes, with approaches such as the Content Extraction via Tag Ratios (CETR) (Weninger et al., 2010) or the Content Extraction via Text Density (CETD) algorithms (Sun et al., 2011). Statistical selection of informative nodes through a combination of both methods proved more efficient on comparable datasets (Qureshi and Memon, 2012). Indeed, the large majority of DOM-based approaches try to leverage semantic information conveyed by HTML tags, notably paragraphs (*p*) on which text-to-tag ratios are calculated (Carey and Manic, 2016). An earlier, language-independent approach uses entropy measures applied to feature, links, and content in order to discriminate among parts of a webpage (Kao et al., 2004).
Machine learning approaches have also been used, whose interest generally consists in leveraging advances in classification tasks by treating a HTML document as a series of blocks to be classified. Relevant algorithms notably include conditional random fields (CRF) learning header, text or noisy blocks using markup-based, content-based, and document-related features (Spousta et al., 2008), support vector machines (SVMs) trained on linguistic, structural and visual features (Bauer et al., 2007), or more recently deep learning, for example with convolutional neural networks (CNNs) learning combinations of DOM-based features (Vogels et al., 2018).
Regarding the evaluation of extraction methods, the Cleaneval dataset and metrics (Baroni et al., 2008) have been used as a reference by numerous studies. Granularity and metrics used can have a real impact on results. Character and word-level metrics can be considered as a sequence, in a bag of words approach, or as a set and then ranked by F-score (Gottron, 2007).
Web text extraction is not a solved task, user experience in general turns web content extraction into an active field of research, resulting from higher download and rendering speeds overall as well as from a growing tendency to inject content from a wide variety of sources, notably through the development of "reader modes" and "distillers"[2] for web browsers which strive to reduce the amount of "Web bloat" (Ghasemisharif et al., 2019). Furthermore, many existing algorithms have become somewhat obsolete due to the rapid changes in web technologies over the last 15 years (Weninger et al., 2016). Web page structure is also constantly evolving from the perspective of standards. HTML 5 was first released in 2008 to provide support for multimedia and graphical elements. This standard also streamlined syntax while retaining backward-compatibility. It also provided ways to tag the semantic content of documents with a granularity unseen before, with new page structure elements such as *main*, *section*, *article*, *header*, *footer*, *aside*, or *nav*. The standard has been gradually integrated into publishing practices and content management systems, while the recommendations still evolve, the current standard being HTML 5.2.[3] In addition, publication systems combining HTML code with embedded JavaScript are on the rise, which also raises the question of "dry" and rendered page code.
Last, there is a disciplinary gap between computer scientists and corpus linguists, both at the time of and following the "web as corpus" paradigm. As well as other research traditions sharing the Web as a research object without communicating much (Brügger and Laursen, 2019), both communities do not seem to be interconnected, although they could benefit from each other's results. We believe content extraction does not get the amount of attention it deserves in the corpus linguistics community. Additionally, precise metadata extraction is paramount in the humanities and remains a collateral issue of this disciplinary gap.

1.3. Contributions

Distinguishing between whole page and essential parts can help to alleviate many quality problems related to web texts. While this is particularly useful in the case of deduplication and studies relying on frequency-based information, other tasks related to content extraction also benefit from a cleaner text base. In the concrete case of linguistic and lexicographic research, it allows for content checks on the only portion of the document that really counts.
In the following, we describe and evaluate text extraction tools published under open-source licenses and whose installation is straightforward. We perform a comparative benchmark on a multilingual setting consisting of real-world data with a manually annotated gold standard. We discuss the results as well as potentially suitable metrics to obtain more fine-grained differentiation. The insights of this paper are thus threefold in terms of software usability, benchmarking, and metrics.

2. Evaluation method

The evaluation described here focuses on integration and real-world usability of the tested solutions. As in previous evaluation campaigns we target the main content, which is usually the part displayed centrally, without the left or right bars, the header or the footer, but including potential titles and comments. We gathered tools coming from different research and industrial backgrounds, different countries, and developed during different time frames.

2.1. Tested solutions

The current benchmark focuses on the Python programming language which is reportedly the most popular programming language in academia[4] and one of the most popular overall. A few algorithms below are adapted from other languages such as Java and JavaScript, which contributes to giving an exhaustive yet incomplete panorama of available solutions overall.
The following tools keep the structure intact but don't focus on main text extraction, they are kept in the benchmark to see how they perform in terms of recall, that is in order to measure how easy it would be to simply gather all the extractable text:

[2] https://chromium.googlesource.com/chromium/dom-distiller
[3] https://www.w3.org/TR/2017/REC-html52-20171214/

[4] https://spectrum.ieee.org/computing/software/the-top-programming-languages-2019

- HTML2TEXT[5] performs text extraction
- INSCRIPTIS[6] converts HTML to text with a particular emphasis on nested tables.

The following tools focus on main text extraction which is the task at hand:

- BOILERPY3[7] is a Python version of the boilerpipe algorithm (Kohlschütter et al., 2010) for boilerplate removal and fulltext extraction;
- DRAGNET[8] works as a meta-classifier using different methods weighted by machine learning (Peters and Lecocq, 2013), it requires more dependencies and potentially fine-tuning or re-training to work at its best;
- GOOSE3[9] can extract information for embedded content but doesn't preserve markup;
- JUSTEXT[10] is designed to preserve mainly text containing full sentences along with some markup, it has been explicitly developed to create linguistic resources (Pomikálek, 2011);
- NEWSPAPER[11] is mostly geared towards newspaper texts, provides additional functions but no structured text or comment extraction
- NEWS-PLEASE[12] is a news crawler that extracts structured information (Hamborg et al., 2017);
- PYTHON-READABILITY[13] is a Python port of the Readability library used in Firefox to display distraction-free webpages, it cleans the page and preserves some markup.

The systems are used out-of-the-box or with minimal fine-tuning. Some of them come from an academic and others from an engineering or commercial background. Some are not being actively developed while others are still being updated. There is no reason to believe some would be disadvantaged as the pages they are tested on are anterior to their development. We use different pre-tuned configurations (here after mode) for the tools that offer this possibility: BOILERPY3 and JUSTEXT. All the code developed for this evaluations is available online.[14]
In the results section we will use the following names for the tools:

- BP3 for BOILERPY3 (default configuration) BP3_Art for the *Article* mode, BP3_KeepE for the *KeepEverything* mode and BP3_Larg for the *Largest* mode;
- DRAG for DRAGNET;
- GOOSE for GOOSE3;
- JT for JUSTEXT (default configuration), JT_en for the *English* mode and JT_langid for the *language dependent* mode;
- NPAPER for NEWSPAPER;
- NPLEASE for NEWS-PLEASE;
- READ for *Python-Readability*.

[5]https://github.com/Alir3z4/html2text/
[6]https://github.com/weblyzard/inscriptis
[7]https://github.com/jmriebold/BoilerPy3
[8]https://github.com/dragnet-org/dragnet
[9]https://github.com/goose3/goose3
[10]https://github.com/miso-belica/jusText
[11]https://github.com/codelucas/newspaper
[12]https://github.com/fhamborg/news-please
[13]https://github.com/buriy/python-readability
[14]https://github.com/rundimeco/waddle

Data	NBlines	NBtokens	NBchar
Html	1385 (±1303)	4726 (±3921)	75015 (±51924)
Clean	13 (±10)	321 (±323)	2296 (±1982)

Table 1: Corpus statistics on the original Html pages and their manually cleaned versions

2.2. Corpus

For our experiments we take advantage of the multilingual, human-annotated corpus DAnIEL, used previously for segmentation and event detection tasks (Lejeune et al., 2012) and extraction (Lejeune and Zhu, 2018). It comprises 1694 documents in five languages: Chinese, English, Greek, Polish and Russian. Each document is present as in its original HTML version and as a cleaned version with the text and some markup. To the best of our knowledge it is the largest multilingual corpus for evaluating web content extraction tools.
The documents have been collected in 2011 and 2012 to evaluate a text classification tool. The HTML 5 standard was not published as a W3C recommendation before 2014, thus it is to be expected that the documents analyzed here almost exclusively ground on HTML 4 which has been a reference since the end of the 1990s.
We wish to compare the results of extrinsic evaluation (e.g. how does the web cleaning tool influence the result of classification) and intrinsic evaluation, e.g. to what extent the extracted content matches the expected outcome. We focus on the latter, not only to find the potentially "best" solution but also to provide more insights on the metrics and results of the evaluation. The dataset is available upon request.
Table 1 shows some statistics on the corpus, the HTML original files and the manually curated clean versions. We can see two different families of tools:

- Recall oriented tools such as HTML2TEXT, INSCRIPTIS and BP3_KEEPE: they tend to extract much more data than expected
- Precision-oriented tools (all the others) which are really devoted to avoid noise.

Table 2 and Table 3 show statistical descriptions of the output for all the tools, as we are looking for misses or near misses. We define almost empty documents as cases where the size of the output represents less than 10% of the size of the clean document. It shows how many times one can

Data	NBlines	NBtokens	NBchar
BP3	22 (±27)	380 (±492)	2656 (±3091)
BP3_Art	16 (±21)	314 (±353)	2287 (±2328)
BP3_KeepE	188 (±133)	1189 (±1009)	8252 (±6363)
BP3_Larg	14 (±22)	285 (±345)	2049 (±2265)
DRAGNET	7 (±10)	252 (±326)	1723 (±2001)
GOOSE	6 (±10)	202 (±297)	1296 (±2091)
HTML2T	335 (±200)	1581 (±1307)	21204 (±13747)
INSCRI	243 (±176)	1409 (±1200)	20649 (±31550)
JT	14 (±17)	381 (±499)	2501 (±3092)
JT_en	6 (±14)	169 (±435)	1008 (±2549)
JT_langid	14 (±17)	376 (±496)	2467 (±3073)
NPAPER	8 (±12)	205 (±314)	1301 (±2015)
NPLEASE	15 (±21)	267 (±361)	1703 (±2277)
READ	35 (±76)	351 (±371)	2932 (±2729)

Table 2: Statistics on the output of the different tools and configurations

Data	el	en	pl	ru	zh
BP3	31.9%	6.9%	2.2%	5.7%	1.0%
BP3_Art	30.8%	6.9%	2.2%	5.3%	0.7%
BP3_KeepE	0.0%	3.6%	0.7%	1.9%	0.0%
BP3_Larg	30.8%	6.9%	2.2%	5.3%	1.0%
DRAGNET	49.1%	1.3%	10.9%	23.2%	3.4%
GOOSE	99.3%	1.5%	11.7%	65.4%	28.0%
HTML2T	0.0%	0.0%	0.0%	0.0%	0.0%
INSCRI	0.0%	0.0%	0.0%	0.0%	0.0%
JT	1.8%	4.2%	0.0%	0.4%	28.7%
JT_en	98.2%	4.2%	99.6%	99.6%	29.2%
JT_langid	1.8%	4.2%	0.0%	0.4%	28.7%
NEWSP	95.2%	1.0%	22.6%	95.4%	29.2%
NEWSP	46.5%	1.3%	5.1%	65.0%	92.9%
READ	0.7%	1.3%	2.2%	0.4%	17.9%

Table 3: Proportion of empty or almost empty ($< 10\%$ of the expected size) files for each language

be sure that the output clearly does not fit the result one can expect from a text extractor. Obviously, the three tools of the recall-oriented family seldom output empty or almost empty files. Most tools seem to be primarily designed for English and not well-adapted to Chinese. We can see the importance of the JUSTEXT language models when compared to the English mode (JT_EN). But the default configuration performs well, except in Chinese for which we had to adapt the configuration[15]. Because of differences in both data sample and processing it is important to choose appropriate metrics which can highlight disparities in tool efficiency. The metrics are described and discussed in the following section.

3. Results

3.1. Processing time

We present in Table 4 the processing time for each tool. There are noticeable differences between them, partly due to the fact that some tools go far beyond a mere text extraction, most notably NEWS-PLEASE. We included this information as it needs to be taken into account for users that need to process data in real time or to clean big datasets but we won't discuss it thoroughly. We can see that DRAGNET and INSCRIPTIS seem to be the fastest systems, whereas language settings for JUSTEXT affect the results significantly.

[15]We followed the recommendations from the author: https://github.com/miso-belica/jusText/issues/12.

Tool	Proc. time	Diff. with fastest
INSCRI	**19.7**	x1
DRAG	24.0	x1.2
BP3_KeepE	37.5	x1.9
BP3_Larg	37.7	x1.9
BP3	38.1	x1.9
BP3_Art	39.8	x2.0
JT_english	41.5	x2.1
READ	56.8	x2.9
HTML2T	71.0	x3.6
NPAPER	105.5	x5.5
JT_langid	112.6	x5.7
GOO	191.3	x9.7
JT	322.0	x16.3
NPLEASE	3755.6	x190

Table 4: Mean execution time over 5 iterations (in seconds) to process the test corpus (1694 documents) on a laptop

3.2. Evaluation Metrics

Since the CLEANEVAL campaigns (Baroni et al., 2008), a state-of-the-art evaluation scheme has been set up and accepted by the community. This metric is based on the following assumption: a text is a sequence of tokens with or without HTML tags and a good content extraction solution should preserve this sequence. The proposition consists in matching the longest common subsequence between a gold standard version of the text and the result given by an extractor. While there are still unmatched zones, the algorithm recursively finds the next longest common subsequence in these zones. The insertion of a sequence not present in the Gold Standard is a False Positive. Conversely, a sequence that is missing in the result of the extractor is a False Negative. This proved to be convenient since classical metrics like recall, precision and f-score can be computed.

However, this metric has some flaws. First of all, it has a quadratic complexity due to the use of the Ratcliff/Obershelp algorithm (Ratcliff and Metzener, 1988). Even on small datasets it is very slow. Secondly, it does not account properly for recall. For instance, copy-pasting the whole content of the document (e.g. with a very naive *html-to-text* tool) does not achieve 100% recall. As a consequence, we propose to use three additional metrics. Let GT be the Ground Truth and RES be the result of a given extractor and GT_{tok} and RES_{tok} be the sequence of their tokens. Let TP be the number of True Positives, FP the number of False Positives and FN the number of False Negatives.

In order to favor comparisons, the tokenization is produced by the exact same code as in CLEANEVAL except for Chinese where a segmentation in characters has been

performed. [16]
The first one, `voc_eval`, simply compares the vocabulary of GT and RE:

- Let GT_{voc} be the set of GT_{tok} and RES_{voc} the set of RES_{tok}
- TP = $|GT_{voc} \cap RES_{voc}|$
- FP = $|RES_{voc} \setminus GT_{voc}|$
- FN = $|GT_{voc} \setminus SET_{voc}|$

The second one, `occ_eval` compares the number of occurrences for each token.

- For each token t in GT_{tok} :
  - $TP = 0, FP = 0, FN = 0$
  - Compute $freq(t_{GT})$ (resp. $freq(t_{RES})$) its frequency in GT (resp. in RES)
  - TP += $min(freq(t_{RES}), freq(t_{GT})$
  - FP += $freq(t_{RES}) - TP$
  - FN += $freq(t_{GT}) - TP$
- For each token u of $RES_{voc} \setminus GT_{voc}$:
  - FP += $freq(t_{RES})$

We also wish to apply other indicators in order to make other types of differences visible among all the tested tools. As such, we opt for two metrics: cosine and euclidean distance. These distances are regularly used for assessing the closeness between two documents (Platt et al., 2010; Buck and Koehn, 2016) , therefore we thought it could yield useful insights in this context.
The last one (`KL_eval`) uses the Kullback-Leibler divergence (a measure of relative entropy between two probability distributions):

- VOC = $GT_{voc} \cup RES_{tok}$ (union of the vocabularies of GT and RES)
- Let P_{gt} (resp. P_{res}) be the probability distribution in GT (resp. RES) of each token of VOC
- for all x in P_{gt} (resp. P_{res}):
  - if $P_{gt}(x) = 0$ (resp.$P_{res}(x) = 0$)
    - $P_{gt}(x) \leftarrow 10^{-5}$ (resp. $P_{res}(x) \leftarrow 10^{-5}$)
- $D_{KL}(P_g \parallel P_{res}) = -\sum_{x\in\mathcal{X}} P(x) \log\left(\frac{P_g(x)}{P_{res}(x)}\right)$

The Kullback-Leibler divergence is not a distance metric since it is not symmetric but it is a way to measure how probability distributions diverge. In our case, we do not need a symmetric measure since we just want to account for the closeness with the GT probability distribution.
The first two metrics allow us to compute recall, precision and f-score whereas `KL_eval` yields a single measure: the smaller the divergence, the greater the similarity of the two documents.

[16]See https://github.com/rundimeco/waddle

3.3. Evaluation on the multilingual corpus

Table 5 lists the results of each tool on the `clean-eval` evaluation scheme. The precision and recall are means, which is important for the interpretation since document-wise evaluation tends to favor systems that do not yield results much smaller that expected. The f-score is the classical version (with $\beta = 1$) computed on the mean precision and mean recall. We could also have chosen to compute a mean of the different f-scores but decided it would be strange to have a geometric mean of harmonic means.
The first thing we can see is that BP3 is very efficient. READABILITY offers a slightly worse result but with a higher recall whereas JUSTEXT exhibits a drop in recall in comparison. DRAGNET has the highest precision score but with a recall below 60%. The recall-oriented tool family leads to lower scores but we can see that INSCRIPTIS is better than HTML2TEXT in both recall and precision. It seems to be a good tool for task when it is important to get as much content as possible.

Tool	f-score	precision	recall
BP3_Art	**78.84**	82.80 (±26)	75.24 (±34)
BP3_Larg	76.44	84.57 (±26)	69.74 (±35)
READ	75.87	72.18 (±28)	79.96 (±27)
BP3	72.83	75.42 (±25)	70.41 (±33)
JT	71.22	78.93 (±25)	64.88 (±41)
JT_langid	70.71	78.96 (±25)	64.02 (±41)
DRAGNET	69.66	**87.53** (±22)	57.85 (±38)
NPLEASE	58.46	69.00 (±41)	50.72 (±45)
GOO	53.93	83.89 (±22)	39.74 (±43)
NPAPER	50.83	82.20 (±22)	36.78 (±44)
BP3_KeepE	47.19	31.74 (±20)	91.97 (±20)
INSCRI	42.95	27.72 (±17)	**95.28** (±13)
JT_en	37.15	79.81 (±21)	24.21 (±39)
HTML2T	33.98	20.86 (±16)	91.47 (±15)

Table 5: Evaluation with the `clean-eval` metric, sorted by descending f-score (computed on the mean precision and the mean recall)

The `clean-eval` measures for the quality of web page cleaning is widely used but it uses a convoluted algorithm relying on the alignment of sequences of words. Its rationale is quite straightforward: nobody wants to have a discontinuous version of the data or to have words in the wrong order. But it appears that in HTML code, the sequence of text blocks is in the same order as the original text. One can see there is not much difference between this evaluation and `occ_eval` (Table 7). There are some differences in ranking concerning the `voc_eval` metric (Table 6. Therefore, we can say that we can use the `occ_eval` metric which has the advantage of being around ten times faster to compute.
Table 8 shows the evaluation with cosine distance, euclidean distance and Kullback-Leibler divergence. Interestingly, this metric seems to be able to highlight systems that show a good balance between silence and noise (like READABILITY and JUSTEXT). Moreover, it does not penalize much systems with large recall scores (like INSCRIPTIS or HTML2TEXT).

Tool	f-score	precision	recall
JT	**75.68**	81.83 (±22)	70.39 (±36)
JT_langid	75.32	81.93 (±22)	69.69 (±35)
BP3_Art	75.30	78.96 (±26)	71.96 (±34)
BP3Larg	73.75	80.94 (±26)	67.74 (±34)
READ	72.52	70.91 (±29)	74.21 (±31)
BP3	71.78	73.22 (±25)	70.40 (±33)
DRAGNET	68.94	86.23 (±22)	57.43 (±36)
NPLEASE	67.28	**92.51** (±17)	52.86 (±44)
GOOSE	60.08	89.51 (±19)	45.21 (±41)
NPAPER	56.78	88.78 (±18)	41.74 (±42)
BP3_KeepE	45.82	30.73 (±22)	90.01 (±20)
INSCRI	45.69	30.56 (±21)	**90.43** (±18)
JT_en	43.57	88.17 (±18)	28.94 (±38)
HTML2T	36.59	23.10 (±17)	87.96 (±18)

Table 6: Evaluation with the `voc_eval` metric

Tool	f-score	precision	recall
BP3_Art	**76.38**	80.60 (±24)	72.57 (±33)
BP3_Larg	74.54	82.90 (±24)	67.72 (±33)
JT	74.13	81.36 (±23)	68.08 (±37)
JT_langid	73.73	81.50 (±23)	67.31 (±37)
READ	73.25	72.43 (±28)	74.09 (±30)
BP3	72.50	74.27 (±24)	70.81 (±32)
DRAGNET	67.09	86.82 (±21)	54.67 (±37)
NPLEASE	66.64	**92.03** (±17)	52.23 (±44)
GOOSE	57.74	89.42 (±19)	42.64 (±42)
NPAPER	54.78	88.68 (±18)	39.63 (±43)
BP3_KeepE	42.02	27.41 (±21)	89.98 (±18)
JT_en	41.35	88.09 (±18)	27.01 (±39)
INSCRI	37.10	23.22 (±18)	**92.22** (±13)
HTML2T	33.45	20.56 (±17)	89.80 (±14)

Table 7: Evaluation with the `occ_eval` metric

This is not surprising since, even with smoothing, this measure tends to favor close probabilities in the same order of magnitude, in other words $P(x) = 1 * 10^{-4}$ is closer to $Q(x) = 3 * 10^{-4}$ than $R(x) = 1 * 10^{-5}$.

3.4. Results by language

The results on the five languages of the corpus describe major discrepancies between the tools. First of all, Table 9 shows the results obtained on English documents with the `clean-eval` metric and Table 10 the results for the `occ_eval` metric. Again, we can see that `occ_eval` yields comparable results. Since it is a simpler measure we will focus on this one for the remainder of the article.

One can see that the scores are much higher than the scores showed in Tables 5 and 7, which highlights that English is a very specific case. Our results demonstrate that most tools are primarily designed to process English documents. Furthermore, the tools that perform very well in this subcorpus are not as efficient on the multilingual corpus. So, one cannot rely on results evaluated solely on English to draw conclusions on the efficiency of a tool in real-world multilingual settings.

Except the three recall-oriented tools, all yield an

Tool	KL div.	Euclidean	Cosine
JT	1.15 (±1.5)	0.17 (±0.2)	**0.12** (±0.1)
BP3_KeepE	1.16 (±1.0)	0.22 (±0.1)	0.36 (±0.2)
JT_langid	1.17 (±1.5)	0.17 (±0.2)	**0.12** (±0.1)
INSCRI	1.18 (±0.7)	0.25 (±0.1)	0.41 (±0.2)
BP3_Art	1.21 (±1.8)	0.15 (±0.2)	0.13 (±0.2)
BP3	1.29 (±1.8)	0.17 (±0.2)	0.15 (±0.2)
HTML2T	1.31 (±0.8)	0.21 (±0.1)	0.41 (±0.2)
BP3_Larg	1.31 (±1.8)	0.15 (±0.2)	0.13 (±0.2)
READ	1.38 (±2.2)	0.17 (±0.3)	0.17 (±0.3)
DRAGNET	1.87 (±2.1)	0.22 (±0.3)	0.19 (±0.2)
GOOSE	2.66 (±2.5)	0.36 (±0.3)	0.26 (±0.3)
NPAPER	2.98 (±2.6)	0.40 (±0.3)	0.29 (±0.3)
NPLEASE	3.36 (±3.6)	0.60 (±0.7)	0.36 (±0.4)
JT_en	3.76 (±2.5)	0.51 (±0.3)	0.36 (±0.3)

Table 8: Evaluation with the `KL_eval` metric, euclidean and cosine distances

Tool	f-score	precision	recall
NPAPER	**90.36**	90.39 (±17)	90.33 (±15)
GOOSE	89.76	**92.01** (±17)	87.62 (±16)
DRAGNET	88.01	87.80 (±21)	88.23 (±19)
NPLEASE	87.83	86.86 (±16)	88.83 (±15)
READ	86.21	83.50 (±19)	89.11 (±16)
BP3_Art	85.95	86.18 (±18)	85.71 (±28)
JT	83.63	82.04 (±23)	85.29 (±25)
BP3_Larg	82.92	87.26 (±20)	78.98 (±30)
JT_langid	82.68	82.03 (±24)	83.34 (±26)
JT_en	82.68	82.03 (±24)	83.34 (±26)
BP3	81.40	77.32 (±20)	85.94 (±26)
BP3_KeepE	52.38	36.36 (±21)	93.65 (±20)
INSCRI	45.74	29.81 (±17)	**98.24** (±4)
HTML2T	44.17	28.70 (±17)	95.82 (±7)

Table 9: Evaluation with the `clean-eval` metric (documents in English) , sorted by descending f-score

`occ_eval` f-score of 80% and higher. NEWSPAPER outperforms the other tools with an f-score above 90%. GOOSE is slightly below and close to NEWSPLEASE but it is much faster (around 35 times according to Table 4). The three tools designed for readability (READABILITY itself but also NEWSPAPER and NEWS-PLEASE) all perform very well.

Table 11 introduces the results on the Greek subcorpus. The three best tools perform comparably to the three top tools for English. It is interesting to see that the language-dependent JUSTEXT configuration yields results comparable to the default configuration. NEWSPAPER, GOOSE and obviously JT_EN perform poorly on this subcorpus. It is obvious for the latter but it is astonishing that the other two do not perform well.

Table 12 shows the results obtained on the Polish subcorpus. We can see that the results are much lower than in English and Greek, both in terms of precision and recall. The best performers on the English subcorpus do not offer comparable results except for NEWSPLEASE andJUSTEXT.

Tool	f-score	precision	recall
NPAPER	**91.32**	91.34 (±16)	91.31 (±14)
GOOSE	90.69	**92.94** (±16)	88.54 (±15)
NPLEASE	88.91	87.89 (±15)	89.96 (±14)
DRAGNET	88.78	88.52 (±19)	89.04 (±18)
READ	87.16	84.31 (±18)	90.21 (±15)
BP3_Art	87.00	87.50 (±17)	86.51 (±28)
JT	84.86	83.16 (±22)	86.62 (±24)
BP3_Larg	84.72	89.14 (±18)	80.73 (±28)
JT_langid	84.08	83.35 (±22)	84.83 (±25)
JT_en	84.08	83.35 (±22)	84.83 (±25)
BP3	82.56	78.46 (±20)	87.11 (±26)
BP3_KeepE	52.66	36.56 (±21)	94.08 (±19)
INSCRI	45.84	29.88 (±17)	**98.46** (±4)
HTML2T	44.61	28.98 (±17)	96.84 (±6)

Table 10: Evaluation with the `occ_eval` metric (documents in English)

Tool	f-score	precision	recall
JT_langid	**88.95**	90.41 (±21)	87.54 (±21)
JT	88.80	89.97 (±21)	87.66 (±21)
READ	86.62	83.03 (±19)	90.54 (±11)
BP3_Art	74.63	88.17 (±19)	64.70 (±44)
BP3_Larg	74.58	89.56 (±18)	63.90 (±43)
BP3	74.17	87.60 (±17)	64.31 (±44)
NPLEASE	65.07	**96.00** (±12)	49.21 (±47)
BP3_KeepE	51.20	34.79 (±16)	96.92 (±5)
INSCRI	50.66	34.21 (±15)	**97.56** (±5)
DRAGNET	43.82	93.94 (±15)	28.57 (±33)
HTML2T	41.03	26.06 (±14)	96.39 (±5)
NPAPER	5.58	92.98 (±18)	2.88 (±12)
GOOSE	2.98	95.11 (±12)	1.51 (±6)
JT_en	2.33	94.10 (±16)	1.18 (±1)

Table 11: Evaluation with the `occ_eval` metric (documents in Greek)

Tool	f-score	precision	recall
BP3_Art	**84.20**	85.11 (±22)	83.32 (±26)
NPLEASE	83.13	86.02 (±21)	80.44 (±29)
JT	82.47	77.71 (±25)	87.85 (±17)
JT_langid	82.15	77.89 (±25)	86.90 (±18)
BP3_Larg	81.40	86.24 (±23)	77.07 (±28)
DRAGNET	79.79	85.84 (±21)	74.54 (±33)
READ	79.23	77.50 (±23)	81.03 (±24)
BP3	78.11	73.03 (±24)	83.96 (±23)
GOOSE	74.84	86.32 (±25)	66.05 (±35)
NPAPER	73.86	85.04 (±21)	65.28 (±41)
BP3_KeepE	48.42	32.69 (±18)	93.35 (±14)
INSCRI	43.28	28.00 (±16)	**95.28** (±11)
HTML2T	36.06	22.45 (±15)	91.57 (±11)
JT_en	1.96	**91.06** (±16)	0.99 (±1)

Table 12: Evaluation with the `occ_eval` metric (documents in Polish)

Tool	f-score	precision	recall
JT	**76.29**	71.64 (±29)	81.59 (±22)
JT_langid	75.99	71.57 (±29)	80.99 (±23)
READ	74.27	72.29 (±27)	76.36 (±26)
BP3_Larg	72.58	77.30 (±31)	68.40 (±34)
BP3_Art	69.31	70.11 (±35)	68.53 (±34)
BP3	66.50	60.82 (±28)	73.34 (±28)
DRAGNET	50.94	85.13 (±27)	36.34 (±31)
NPLEASE	42.64	93.16 (±20)	27.64 (±41)
GOOSE	40.24	90.96 (±21)	25.83 (±38)
BP3_KeepE	36.93	23.30 (±20)	88.89 (±19)
INSCRI	32.53	19.77 (±16)	**91.75** (±17)
HTML2T	29.55	17.63 (±14)	91.35 (±14)
NPAPER	5.14	92.34 (±19)	2.64 (±9)
JT_en	3.55	**95.37** (±12)	1.81 (±6)

Table 13: Evaluation with the `occ_eval` metric (documents in Russian)

Tool	f-score	precision	recall
BP3_Art	**63.30**	71.28 (±24)	56.93 (±22)
BP3_Larg	57.95	72.53 (±24)	48.26 (±22)
BP3	55.20	70.08 (±25)	45.53 (±19)
DRAGNET	44.53	81.81 (±23)	30.59 (±18)
READ	42.36	48.00 (±32)	37.91 (±28)
GOOSE	20.60	82.54 (±17)	11.77 (±9)
JT_langid	19.19	82.32 (±17)	10.86 (±5)
JT	19.19	82.32 (±17)	10.86 (±5)
JT_en	19.18	82.80 (±17)	10.84 (±5)
NPAPER	19.17	82.72 (±17)	10.84 (±5)
BP3_KeepE	19.08	10.85 (±15)	78.94 (±18)
HTML2T	13.83	7.62 (±11)	74.87 (±15)
NPLEASE	13.31	**97.52** (±12)	7.14 (±13)
INSCRI	12.97	7.06 (±10)	**79.52** (±14)

Table 14: Evaluation with the `occ_eval` metric (documents in Chinese), evaluation by character n-grams

It seems harder to extract text from Russian pages since no system is able to achieve above 80% f-score (Table 13). Again, JUSTEXT is among the best performers. Contrary to the Polish subcorpus, it is BP3_Larg that is the best BP3 configuration. We can see again that READABILITY performs very well on other languages than English.
Finally, the worst results are related to the Chinese subcorpus (Table 14). BP3 outperforms the rest of the field by far. One can see that the choice of a tool is much more important for Chinese than for English since many tools result in f-scores below 20%. We can note that it is the only language for which INSCRIPTIS does not achieve 90% recall.

3.5. Is there a winner?

The results we presented yield differentiated insights so that it is difficult to give a definitive and universal answer. First of all, if one targets recall and/or speed INSCRIPTIS is clearly the most efficient solution. In general BP3 and READABILITY are the most stable systems and the only ones that perform reasonably well for Chinese.

If we do not consider Chinese, JUSTEXT in its language-independent setting seems to be the most efficient solution for multilingual corpora. That being said, this setting is much slower and it is not strictly comparable as it uses additional information but most of all it does not appear to perform better. For texts in English GOOSE and NEWSPAPER outperform the other systems. For Polish, BP3_ART shows a comparable f-score than JUSTEXT but with a better precision. For Russian BP3_LARG is a good solution if one needs precision but JUSTEXT achieves a satisfying trade-off between precision and recall. According to our study, there appears to be no benefit from more intricate machine-learning approaches, DRAGNET does not stand out and does not perform poorly either. However, the amount of additional training data needed to potentially improve its results is a penalty in terms of usability compared to the other solutions for which parameter tuning could lead to improvements much faster. JUSTEXT is such an example where changing settings can be done easily.

4. Conclusions and outlook

The article focused on a comparative benchmark of open-source tools used on web documents from 2011 and 2012 written in five different languages, along with a discussion of suitable metrics. Content processing is affected by both diatopic and diachronic factors, whereas vocabulary analysis and distance metrics can yield more fine-grained information which complements the CLEANEVAL evaluation standard. Rule-based approaches appear to be more efficient in the long run, all the more since they are both easier to use and to parametrize.

Most tools are developed with particular page styles in mind, mostly from the English-speaking world. Our data shows that linguistic factors are most probably reflected in HTML structures, which deeply affects extraction processes. The experiments above highlight the diversity of layouts and web coding practices depending on language and most probably on the country from which a document is published. These discrepancies are reflected by diverging performances so that the right tool has to be chosen accordingly.

In addition, different eras of web development result in diverging "HTMLects". Our corpus provides a snapshot of a past version of the Web which proves to be challenging for some tools. As such, it is useful to assess how data from Web archives can be processed. These findings prompt for further studies on the evaluation of tool robustness with respect to the ever-changing Web. We have reasons to believe that the success of standardized publishing platforms and the consecutive advent of HTML 5 changes the way text is published on the Web, all of which could pave the way for further examinations.

5. References

Bar-Yossef, Z. and Rajagopalan, S. (2002). Template Detection via Data Mining and its Applications. In *Proceedings of the 11th International Conference on World Wide Web*, pages 580–591.

Barbaresi, A. (2015). *Ad hoc and general-purpose corpus construction from web sources*. Ph.D. thesis, École Normale Supérieure de Lyon.

Barbaresi, A. (2016). Efficient construction of metadata-enhanced web corpora. In Paul Cook, et al., editors, *Proceedings of the 10th Web as Corpus Workshop*, pages 7–16. Association for Computational Linguistics.

Barbaresi, A. (2019). The Vast and the Focused: On the need for thematic web and blog corpora. In Piotr Bański, et al., editors, *Proceedings of the CMLC-7 workshop*, pages 29–32.

Baroni, M., Chantree, F., Kilgarriff, A., and Sharoff, S. (2008). Cleaneval: a Competition for Cleaning Web Pages. In *Proceedings of LREC*, pages 638–643. ELRA.

Baroni, M., Bernardini, S., Ferraresi, A., and Zanchetta, E. (2009). The WaCky Wide Web: a collection of very large linguistically processed web-crawled corpora. *Language Resources and Evaluation*, 43(3):209–226.

Bauer, D., Degen, J., Deng, X., Herger, P., Gasthaus, J., Giesbrecht, E., Jansen, L., Kalina, C., Kräger, T., Märtin, R., Schmidt, M., Scholler, S., Steger, J., Stemle, E., and Evert, S. (2007). FIASCO: Filtering the internet by automatic subtree classification. In *Building and Exploring Web Corpora: Proceedings of the 3rd Web as Corpus Workshop (WAC-3)*, pages 111–121.

Brügger, N. and Laursen, D. (2019). Introduction: Digital humanities, the web, and national web domains. In *The Historical Web and Digital Humanities*, pages 1–9. Routledge.

Buck, C. and Koehn, P. (2016). Quick and reliable document alignment via TF/IDF-weighted cosine distance. In *Proceedings of the First Conference on Machine Translation: Volume 2, Shared Task Papers*, pages 672–678, Berlin, Germany, August. Association for Computational Linguistics.

Cai, D., Yu, S., Wen, J.-R., and Ma, W.-Y. (2003). VIPS: a Vision-based Page Segmentation Algorithm. Technical report, Microsoft Research.

Carey, H. J. and Manic, M. (2016). HTML web content extraction using paragraph tags. In *25th International Symposium on Industrial Electronics (ISIE)*, pages 1099–1105. IEEE.

Geyken, A., Barbaresi, A., Didakowski, J., Jurish, B., Wiegand, F., and Lemnitzer, L. (2017). Die Korpusplattform des "Digitalen Wörterbuchs der deutschen Sprache" (DWDS). *Zeitschrift für germanistische Linguistik*, 45(2):327–344.

Ghasemisharif, M., Snyder, P., Aucinas, A., and Livshits, B. (2019). SpeedReader: Reader Mode Made Fast and Private. In *Proceedings of the World Wide Web Conference*, pages 526–537.

Gottron, T. (2007). Evaluating content extraction on HTML documents. In *Proceedings of the 2nd International Conference on Internet Technologies and Applications*, pages 123–132.

Gupta, S., Kaiser, G., Neistadt, D., and Grimm, P. (2003). DOM-based content extraction of HTML documents. In *Proceedings of the 12th international conference on World Wide Web*, pages 207–214.

Habernal, I., Zayed, O., and Gurevych, I. (2016).

C4Corpus: Multilingual Web-size corpus with free license. In *Proceedings of the Tenth International Conference on Language Resources and Evaluation (LREC'16)*, pages 914–922.

Hamborg, F., Meuschke, N., Breitinger, C., and Gipp, B. (2017). news-please: A generic news crawler and extractor. In Maria Gaede, et al., editors, *Proceedings of the 15th International Symposium of Information Science*, pages 218–223.

Kao, H.-Y., Lin, S.-H., Ho, J.-M., and Chen, M.-S. (2004). Mining web informative structures and contents based on entropy analysis. *IEEE Transactions on Knowledge and Data Engineering*, 16(1):41–55.

Kilgarriff, A. (2007). Googleology is bad science. *Computational Linguistics*, 33(1):147–151.

Kohlschütter, C. and Nejdl, W. (2008). A Densitometric Approach to Web Page Segmentation. In *Proceedings of the 17th ACM Conference on Information and Knowledge Management*, pages 1173–1182.

Kohlschütter, C., Fankhauser, P., and Nejdl, W. (2010). Boilerplate detection using shallow text features. In *Proceedings of the Third ACM International Conference on Web Search and Data Mining, WSDM '10*, pages 441–450.

Lejeune, G. and Zhu, L. (2018). A New Proposal for Evaluating Web Page Cleaning Tools. *Computación y Sistemas*, 22(4).

Lejeune, G., Brixtel, R., Doucet, A., and Lucas, N. (2012). Daniel: Language independent character-based news surveillance. In *International Conference on NLP*, pages 64–75. Springer.

Peters, M. E. and Lecocq, D. (2013). Content extraction using diverse feature sets. In *Proceedings of the 22nd International Conference on World Wide Web*, pages 89–90.

Platt, J., Toutanova, K., and Yih, W.-t. (2010). Translingual document representations from discriminative projections. In *Proceedings of the 2010 Conference on Empirical Methods in Natural Language Processing*, pages 251–261, Cambridge, MA, October. Association for Computational Linguistics.

Pomikálek, J. (2011). *Removing boilerplate and duplicate content from web corpora*. Ph.D. thesis, Masaryk University.

Qureshi, P. A. R. and Memon, N. (2012). Hybrid model of content extraction. *Journal of Computer and System Sciences*, 78(4):1248–1257.

Rae, A. R., Kim, J., Le, D., and Thoma, G. R. (2018). Main Content Detection in HTML Journal Articles. In *Proceedings of the ACM Symposium on Document Engineering 2018*, pages 1–4, New York, NY, USA. ACM.

Ratcliff, J. W. and Metzener, D. E. (1988). Pattern Matching: The Gestalt Approach. *Dr. Dobb's Journal*, 13(7):46.

Schäfer, R., Barbaresi, A., and Bildhauer, F. (2013). The Good, the Bad, and the Hazy: Design Decisions in Web Corpus Construction. In *Proceedings of the 8th Web as Corpus Workshop*, pages 7–15.

Schäfer, R., Barbaresi, A., and Bildhauer, F. (2014). Focused Web Corpus Crawling. In *Proceedings of the 9th Web as Corpus workshop (WAC-9)*, pages 9–15.

Schäfer, R. (2016). CommonCOW: Massively Huge Web Corpora from CommonCrawl Dataand a Method to Distribute them Freely under Restrictive EU Copyright Laws. In *Proceedings of the 10th International Conference on Language Resources and Evaluation (LREC'16)*, pages 4500–4504.

Spousta, M., Marek, M., and Pecina, P. (2008). Victor: the Web-Page Cleaning Tool. In *4th Web as Corpus Workshop (WAC-4)*, pages 12–17.

Sun, F., Song, D., and Liao, L. (2011). DOM-based content extraction via text density. In *Proceedings of the 34th international ACM SIGIR conference on Research and development in Information Retrieval*, pages 245–254.

Vogels, T., Ganea, O.-E., and Eickhoff, C. (2018). Web2text: Deep structured boilerplate removal. In *European Conference on Information Retrieval*, pages 167–179. Springer.

Weninger, T., Hsu, W. H., and Han, J. (2010). CETR: content extraction via tag ratios. In *Proceedings of the 19th international conference on World Wide Web*, pages 971–980.

Weninger, T., Palacios, R., Crescenzi, V., Gottron, T., and Merialdo, P. (2016). Web Content Extraction – a Meta-Analysis of its Past and Thoughts on its Future. *ACM SIGKDD Explorations Newsletter*, 17(2):17–23.

Proceedings of the 12th Web as Corpus Workshop, pages 14–22
Language Resources and Evaluation Conference (LREC 2020), Marseille, 11–16 May 2020

From Web Crawl to Clean Register-Annotated Corpora

Veronika Laippala, Samuel Rönnqvist, Saara Hellström, Juhani Luotolahti
Liina Repo, Anna Salmela, Valtteri Skantsi and Sampo Pyysalo
Turku NLP Group, University of Turku, Turku, Finland
{mavela,saanro,sherik,mjluot,tlkrep,annsalm,valtteri.skantsi,sampo.pyysalo}@utu.fi

Abstract

The web presents unprecedented opportunities for large-scale collection of text in many languages. However, two critical steps in the development of web corpora remain challenging: the identification of clean text from source HTML and the assignment of genre or register information to the documents. In this paper, we evaluate a multilingual approach to this end. Our starting points are the Swedish and French Common Crawl datasets gathered for the 2017 CoNLL shared task, particularly the URLs. We 1) fetch HTML pages based on the URLs and run boilerplate removal, 2) train a classifier to further clean out undesired text fragments, and 3) annotate text registers. We compare boilerplate removal against the CoNLL texts, and find an improvement. For the further cleaning of undesired material, the best results are achieved using Multilingual BERT with monolingual fine-tuning. However, our results are promising also in a cross-lingual setting, without fine-tuning on the target language. Finally, the register annotations show that most of the documents belong to a relatively small set of registers which are relatively similar in the two languages. A number of additional flags in the annotation are, however, necessary to reflect the wide range of linguistic variation associated with the documents.

Keywords: Register, genre, web-as-corpus, boilerplate removal, web data, web scraping

1. Introduction

Traditionally, linguistic corpora are collected in order to represent a language or a specific part of it (McEnery and Wilson, 1996; Biber et al., 1998; Kytö and Ludeling, 2008). Typically, in order to do so, corpora are composed of texts chosen to represent different genres or *registers*, that is, situationally defined text varieties such as news, blogs or discussion forum comments (Biber, 1988). Many web-based language resources diverge from this process by not being based on detailed compilation criteria (see, however, Schäfer (2016c)). Instead of the collection of coherent, high-quality text, the construction of web language resources commonly emphasizes gathering as much data as possible, for instance by using a dedicated crawl or extracting data from existing crawl-based datasets, such as Common Crawl[1]. As crawling and compilation pipelines are based on automatic processes, the resulting data can contain boilerplate texts, machine translations, and even text in languages other than that targeted in the corpus construction. Furthermore, there is typically no information on the kinds of registers that the web language resources represent. Although both linguistic and NLP efforts have achieved significant advances using web data (e.g. Mikolov et al. (2013), Bojanowski et al. (2017), Yang et al. (2019)), for a number of end uses, better structured web language resources with clean, full texts and register information would be essential to realizing their full potential.

Currently, a number of large web-crawled datasets are available. However, resources emphasizing the collection of clean texts, such as WaCky (Baroni et al., 2009) and COW (Schäfer, 2016b), represent only a limited number of languages. The ones with a more extensive selection of languages, such as OSCAR (Ortiz Suárez et al., 2019), have not gone through detailed text cleaning processes. Moreover, register information or further NLP processing steps such as syntactic analysis is typically not included at all.

In this paper, we present efforts toward the automatic creation of multilingual web-based language resources that consist of coherent, clean texts and include similar metadata to what traditional language resources have, in particular registers identified using a detailed, systematic register hierarchy. By *coherent texts*, we understand texts where each text part is linked to the others to form a full, meaningful whole (Halliday, 1976).

Our starting point is the Common Crawl dataset gathered for the 2017 CoNLL shared task (Ginter et al., 2017). Altogether, the dataset includes 56 languages, but in this paper, we focus on the Swedish and French collections. We 1) fetch pages from the URLs found in the collections and run boilerplate removal on the raw HTML, 2) train a classifier to further remove undesired text fragments that may remain, and 3) annotate text registers. The registers, such as *News report* or *Description with intent to sell*, are annotated using the taxonomy presented for English by Egbert et al. (2015) and also applied in Finnish by Laippala et al. (2019). To evaluate the need for boilerplate removal, we compare three versions of the data that have gone through different cleaning processes: 1) texts as included in the CoNLL collections, 2) raw texts after simple removal of markup from the fetched HTML pages, and 3) texts from the HTML pages cleaned of boilerplate and other unwanted elements using the web scraping tool Trafilatura[2]. The process is described in Figure 1.

We make all the resources introduced in this effort freely available under open licences at `https://github.com/TurkuNLP/WAC-XII`.

2. Related work

Web-based language resources are widely applied both in linguistic and NLP research. The WaCky Corpus Collection (Baroni et al., 2009) with more than a billion words in

[1] `https://commoncrawl.org`

[2] `https://github.com/adbar/trafilatura`

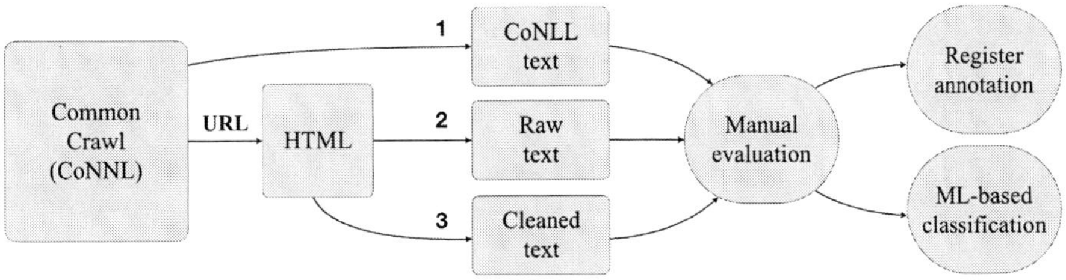

Figure 1: Text preprocessing and annotation process. Three versions of text are manually evaluated: 1) texts taken directly from the CoNLL version of Common Crawl that have undergone a cleaning process, 2) raw texts extracted from HTML based on the CoNLL URLs, and 3) texts extracted from CoNLL URLs by the boilerplate removal system (Trafilatura)

English, French, Italian and German was one of the earliest ones and perhaps mainly targeted at research questions in linguistics. Similarly, the COW corpora (Schäfer, 2016b) are linguistically processed and include billions of words in six European languages. CommonCrawl is a free and openly available web crawl maintained by the CommonCrawl foundation. The dataset is available at Amazon EC2-cloud as both plain text and HTML. The data totals petabytes in size. Lately the Common Crawl dataset has been used to gather text corpora for a number of NLP projects, such as the recently introduced massive multilingual corpus OSCAR (Ortiz Suárez et al., 2019).

An important part of processing web-based datasets for use in linguistic and NLP research is the extraction of the main body of the text and the removal of boilerplate text, such as lists, links and other unwanted material. These decrease the quality of the data as they brake the coherence of the texts by not including full sentences and by presenting individual, repetitive segments such as copyright indications. In the existing web-based language resources, the cleaning process is performed in different ways. The WaCkies (Baroni et al., 2009) use regular expressions and heuristic rules to remove boilerplates. The heuristics are based on the idea that HTML tags co-occur frequently with boilerplates, whereas the document parts with low HTML tag density belong often to main text body. Cow corpora (Schäfer et al., 2013) are processed based on a detailed pipeline with a tool classifying paragraphs as boilerplate or not (Schäfer, 2016a) and a another one classifying entire documents as coherent text or not (Schäfer et al., 2013). These are based on manually annotated data and a document-level unsupervised method to evaluate the text quality based on short and very frequent words. To create the monolingual OSCAR subcorpora, Ortiz Suárez et al. (2019) processed Common Crawl data using a pipeline based on the system by Grave et al. (2018), which included language detection using fastText (Joulin et al., 2016), basic heuristic cleaning, and hashing-based deduplication, but no boilerplate removal.

A number of readily available boilerplate removal packages exist. JusText[3] is a frequently applied boilerplate removal package in python. Trafilatura[4] is a recently developed web-scraping python library that preserves also some of the web page structure. According to an evaluation included

[3] `https://pypi.org/project/jusText/`

[4] `https://trafilatura.readthedocs.io/en/latest/`

Language	Documents	Tokens
French	18.2 million	10.5 billion
Swedish	19.4 million	7.7 billion

Table 1: Sizes of the deduplicated CoNLL 2017 Common Crawl-based datasets for French and Swedish

in its documentation,[5] Trafilatura achieves an accuracy of 91% and outperforms a number of similar tools, including jusText.

Thus, several well-developed web corpus resources and ready-made solutions for boilerplate removal and text cleaning exist. In contrast, the addition of register information to web-scale corpora is not yet common practice and involves many challenges. A first challenge has been the lack of annotated corpora that represent all the registers found online. Because of this, there has been no training data available to develop web register identification systems that could be applied to classify web-based language resources. Two large corpora with register annotations exist for English, the Leeds Web Genre Corpus (Asheghi et al., 2016) and the Corpus of Online Registers of English (CORE) (Egbert et al., 2015). A small collection of online registers has also been released for Finnish (Laippala et al., 2019). Second, another challenge with online registers is that online language use cannot necessarily be described in terms of discrete register categories. For instance, an online text might simultaneously have characteristics of a news article and a persuasive text. Thus, discrete register classification systems where each document belongs to exactly one register category do not necessarily suit web data sets very well. To solve this, the CORE corpus includes *hybrid* register categories that combine several register labels, such as *narrative+opinion* (see Biber and Egbert (2018)). Another solution is suggested by Sharoff (2018), who analyzes registers by describing texts based on proportions of dimensions, such as argumentative or hard news.

3. Data and annotation

In this section, we present the CoNLL data we use as source, the preprocessing steps we applied, and the annotation processes we performed. The overall workflow is presented in Figure 1.

[5] `https://trafilatura.readthedocs.io/en/latest/evaluation.html`

Label	Text
1	Prinsessan Madeleine besökte Childhood-projekt i Florida och New York - Sveriges Kungahus 'Princess Madeleine visited Childhood projects in Florida and New York - The Swedish Royal Court'
0	Länk till sidan Anpassa webbplatsen 'Link to the site Customize the Web Site'
0	Länk till Startsidan 'Link to the home page'

Table 2: Example of text quality annotation for Swedish data. Lines marked with the label 1 are judged to be part of the main body of the text.

3.1. Source data

The source data for our study is gathered from the Common Crawl-based dataset prepared for the 2017 CoNLL shared task (Ginter et al., 2017). The Common Crawl data is available on the Amazon cloud, which was used for data collection and language detection. The Compact Language Detect 2 (CLD2) language detector[6] was applied in processing due to its speed and the availability of python bindings. For each processed plain text input file, the first 100 000 tokens per language were kept, and deduplication based on URLs was performed. The resulting dataset is composed of altogether 56 languages and nearly 100 billion words. The statistics of the French and Swedish collections used in this study are summarized in Table 1.

3.2. Text quality annotation

We evaluate the quality of texts by manually annotating three text versions that have gone through different cleaning processes: 1) text as they are included in the CoNLL data, 2) raw texts extracted from HTML source without boilerplate removal, and 3) texts extracted from HTML and processed with Trafilatura to remove boilerplate material. The raw texts are included in order to assess whether any good text content may have been lost and to provide an up-to-date point of reference for Trafilatura, as some of the online documents may have changed after the collection of the original source data in 2017.

The evaluation was done by 1) selecting from CoNLL data 40 documents (20 in Swedish and 20 in French) with active URLs and 2) manually annotating the quality of all three versions of these documents. The annotation was done on a line-by-line basis, coding which lines are part of the coherent texts and which are part of boilerplate.[7] To define boilerplate, we followed Schäfer (2016a), according to whom boilerplate is all material that "*remains after markup stripping, and which does not belong to one of those blocks of content on the web page that contain coherent text.*"

The annotation was performed by four annotators in total. Annotations were done individually, but difficult cases were discussed jointly with an annotation coordinator. Although many lines and text segments are easy to define as not belonging to the coherent text, the quality annotation was by no means a trivial task. Many lines could have been defined as either coherent text or boilerplate. Examples of undesired lines include links and lists of words or headlines that were not connected to body text, e.g., when serving as links to other pages. Automatically generated text was similarly excluded, e.g., headlines in a banner, phrases such as *visa mer* 'show more' and *fäll ihop* 'hide'.

Table 2 shows examples of lines annotated as belonging to the text and lines annotated as undesired material. The first line is a headline describing the text to come and its topic: the visit of the Princess Madeleine of Sweden. As this headline is not followed by other headlines, it is considered as belonging to the coherent text. The next two lines, in turn, are both links to other parts of the website. They do not belong to the coherent text and are thus annotated as undesired material to be rejected.

[6]https://github.com/CLD2Owners/cld2

[7]Lines correspond broadly to blocks of text uninterrupted by tags in the source HTML, such as titles or paragraphs.

Narrative
News report / news blog, sports report, personal blog, historical article, fiction, travel blog, community blog, online article
Opinion
Review, opinion blog, religious blogs/sermon, advice
Informational Description
Description of a thing, encyclopedia article, research article, description of a person, information blog, FAQ, course material, legal terms / condition, report, job description
Discussion
Discussion forum, question-answer forum
How-to
How-to/instruction, recipe
Informational Persuasion
Description with intent to sell, news+opinion blog / editorial
Lyrical
Songs, poem
Spoken
Interview, formal speech, TV transcript

Table 3: Register classes in the taxonomy. Main register classes are shown in bold.

3.3. Register annotation

The register-annotated documents are sampled from the CoNLL data. The register annotation follows the register taxonomy presented for the English CORE corpus by Egbert et al. (2015) and for Finnish by Laippala et al. (2019). The advantage of this taxonomy is that it is developed in a data-driven manner and it covers the full range of registers and linguistic variation found online. Furthermore, as discussed in Section 2., the annotation allows the assignment of multiple register labels for one document, which guarantees that the annotation covers the full range of language use in web documents. The taxonomy is hierarchical with eight main register classes with functional labels. These are divided into a number of sub-register categories that are perhaps more intuitive, such as *News report* and *Review*. The taxonomy is presented in Table 3.

In the English CORE for which this taxonomy was developed, each document was annotated by four coders, and hybrid annotations resulted from consistent disagreements among the coders. In our study, we do not have the resources to have such an extensive annotation process. Instead, documents were first double-annotated, and when a certain level of agreement and confidence was found between the coders, the process was changed to single annotation. However, difficult cases were always discussed and resolved jointly. In our setting, during the annotation, annotators could select several register labels for a document when necessary to fully characterize it. This allows the direct annotation of hybrid documents even by a single annotator. Moreover, if the document could not be described by a specific sub-register label, annotators could select a more general, main register label only. The annotations were done using a custom annotation tool. The tool provides annotators with a wide selection of flags that can be toggled to identify additional aspects of the texts. The set of flags was developed during the annotation with the objective of marking text properties that may have an effect on the further analysis of the data. For instance, these include *untypical for the register* and *multiple texts*.

French	Accept	Reject
Words	8374 (52%)	7789 (48%)
Lines	288 (23%)	956 (77%)

Swedish	Accept	Reject
Words	20694 (78%)	5961 (22%)
Lines	495 (31%)	1110 (69%)

Table 4: Text quality for CoNLL source text.

French	Accept	Reject
Words	8097 (36%)	14662 (64%)
Lines	408 (9%)	4227 (91%)

Swedish	Accept	Reject
Words	17228 (39%)	27324 (61%)
Lines	568 (11%)	4809 (89%)

Table 5: Text quality for raw text.

French	Accept	Reject
Words	6401 (79%)	1713 (21%)
Lines	306 (55%)	255 (45%)

Swedish	Accept	Reject
Words	12224 (94%)	794 (6%)
Lines	403 (84%)	77 (16%)

Table 6: Text quality for Trafilatura-processed text.

4. Classifiers for further cleaning

We next describe our approach to training and evaluating methods for further cleaning the texts after boilerplate removal. We experiment with two supervised machine learning methods:

BERT (Devlin et al., 2018) is a deep transfer learning approach based on the Transformer architecture (Vaswani et al., 2017). We apply the Multilingual BERT (mBERT) model released by Google[8], which has been pre-trained on a combination of Wikipedia texts in 104 languages, including French and Swedish. In addition to monolingual classification in the two languages, we apply mBERT also in multilingual and cross-lingual training setups. Following Devlin et al. (2018), we add a final classification layer to the pre-trained transformer stack, and fine-tune all model weights.

fastText (Joulin et al., 2016) is a text classification tool emphasizing computational efficiency, making it a popular choice for machine learning on web-scale data. We apply fastText as a baseline method using the supervised text classification facilities of the tool.

We train and evaluate BERT and fastText in the basic binary classification setting where each line is labelled as either 0 (rejected) or 1 (accepted). We divide both the French and the Swedish datasets into training, development, and test subsets on the document level, so that text drawn from a single document is only included in exactly one of the subsets. We perform a random stratified split so that the positive/negative distribution of each subset roughly matches that of the whole dataset (max. 2% point deviation). The test subsets were held out during method development and parameter selection.

For BERT, we perform a grid search on maximum sequence length, learning rate, batch size and number of training epochs, while evaluating on the development set. For fastText, we select the maximum number of word n-grams and the number of training epochs using grid search on the development data. We additionally evaluate the effect of initializing the word vectors for the method using pre-trained language-specific word vectors (Grave et al., 2018).

We evaluate classification performance primarily in terms of accuracy, i.e. the proportion of texts that are predicted to have the correct class. We additionally report precision and recall, summarizing performance across different classification thresholds with precision-recall curves.

5. Results

In this section, we present the results of the evaluations. We start with the analysis of the text quality based on the manual annotations, then move on to the machine learning experiments to further clean the texts from undesired material, and finally analyze the register annotations.

[8] `https://github.com/google-research/bert/blob/master/multilingual.md`

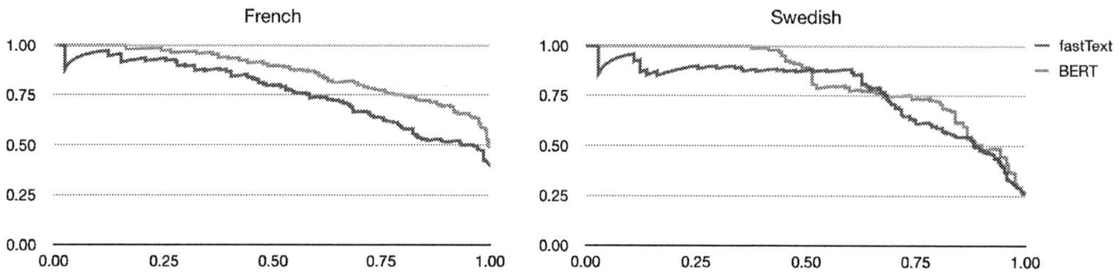

Figure 2: Precision-recall curves for the two machine learning methods. (x-axis: recall, y-axis: precision)

5.1. Text quality based on the manual annotations

The results on the manual evaluation of the text quality are presented in Table 4 for the CoNLL texts, in Table 5 for the raw text, and in Table 6 for the text processed with Trafilatura to remove boilerplate (see Section 3.2.). In the source CoNLL data, 48% of the words in French and 22% of the words in Swedish were evaluated as rejected, i.e., they appeared on lines that were not considered to belong to the coherent texts. On the line level, the proportions were even more drastic: in Swedish, 69% of the lines and in French 77% were marked as rejected. These findings suggest that the source texts may be too noisy to be used without further cleaning for many purposes and that the quality of the French CoNLL data is somewhat lower than that of the Swedish data. Moreover, the different distributions indicate that length is already a strong signal of the line belonging to the coherent text. This seems natural, as many of the short lines enumerating links are very short.

In the raw text versions extracted from HTML, the proportion of words evaluated as not belonging to the coherent texts was 64% in French and 61% in Swedish. On the line level, the rejected proportions were approximately 90% for both languages. Thus, despite its issues, the CoNLL data is clearly cleaner and of better quality than text extracted directly from HTML.

For Trafilatura, the proportions of rejected material were clearly lower than in the other settings. On the word level, the Swedish contained only 6% of rejections and the French 21%, while on the line level, the proportions were 16% and 45% (resp.). Text processed with Trafilatura is thus cleaner than the CoNLL data, and its use is motivated even if the CoNLL data has already gone through some cleaning. On the other hand, the Trafilatura cleaning process does also discard some parts of the raw text that were evaluated as belonging to the text. For Swedish, 5004 words – approximately 29% of accepted words in the raw text extracted from HTML – were deleted by Trafilatura. Similarly, in, French, 1696 accepted words, that is, 21%, were deleted. Thus, obtaining cleaner text in this way also has the downside of not acquiring all the text available. Whether this trade-off is acceptable is likely to depend on the purpose for which the text is processed.

5.2. Classifiers for further cleaning

The machine learning results are based on altogether 50+50 documents from the CoNLL data: 20+20 as described in Table 4 and an additional set of 30+30 documents we annotated in order to guarantee high system performance. Table 7 summarizes the key statistics of the training, development, and test division of the data.

French	Train	Dev	Test	Total
Lines	2437	673	696	3806
Words	44529	15415	11636	71580
Positives	908	253	274	1435
Negatives	1530	421	423	2374

Swedish	Train	Dev	Test	Total
Lines	2867	788	806	4461
Words	37855	9286	10007	57148
Positives	812	222	212	1246
Negatives	2056	567	595	3218

Table 7: Data statistics. Positives refer to the accepted lines annotated as part of the coherent texts, while negatives are the rejected lines annotated as undesired material.

We set machine learning method parameters in a monolingual setting by optimizing the hyperparameters for French and Swedish separately on the development subsets. For mBERT, we found the optimal hyperparameter settings to be largely in agreement across the two languages: both models use a maximum sequence length of 192, batch size of 16 and are trained for 6 epochs. The Swedish model was trained with a learning rate of $2.5e^{-6}$ and the French with $5.0e^{-6}$. For fastText, we selected word n-grams up to length three and training for 30 epochs, initializing the word vectors randomly as pre-initialized vectors did not show a clear benefit in evaluation on the development data. The final evaluation results on the test sets are shown in Table 8. Both fastText and mBERT clearly outperform the majority baseline, and mBERT achieves the best results for both languages, with a more notable advantage for the French data, reaching an accuracy of 85.62% for French and 81.64% for Swedish. Figure 2 shows the precision-recall curves for the two methods. We find that mBERT systematically outperforms fastText across the entire recall range for French, but dips below the precision of fastText for part of the scale for Swedish.

We continued to explore whether training the better-performing method, mBERT, on data combining annotations from both languages could further improve performance, evaluating on each language separately. The multilingual model was trained with the above settings, and the

	French	Swedish
mBERT	**81.64**	**85.62**
fastText	75.68	84.61
Majority	60.69	73.73

Table 8: Monolingual classification accuracy.

	Test	
Train	French	Swedish
French	**81.64**	76.61
Swedish	69.72	**85.62**
Fr + Sv	79.34	82.28

Table 9: Cross- and multilingual classification accuracy with mBERT. Monolingual results are repeated for reference.

learning rate of $2.5e^{-6}$ was found to perform best on the development set. Despite the increase in training data size, the multilingual model falls behind its monolingual counterparts by 2-3% points on the two languages (Table 9).

Finally, we assessed how well the monolingually trained classifiers perform in a zero-shot, cross-lingual learning setting, i.e., how well they can predict in a language not seen during fine-tuning. While we observed a 5% point drop for Swedish, the drop was 16% points for French (Table 9). Nevertheless, both models manage to outperform the majority baseline even in this setting. This is encouraging for the multilingual long-term objective of our project, as it shows that machine learning-based text cleaning is possible even without language-specific training data.

5.3. Large-scale identification of coherent text

Finally, we apply the developed classifiers to a large body of unannotated texts to further assess the ratio of clean text in the source data. In the French and Swedish CoNLL data, we randomly sample URLs from which we then extract the texts using Trafilatura. The process is continued until we reach 10,000 lines in each language.

We classify these lines using the French and Swedish monolingually tuned mBERT models described above, and observe the class proportions as summarized in Table 10. Both languages exhibit a similar distribution – about 27–29% of lines are accepted by the models – while in terms of number of words the ratios are close to the inverse. Somewhat less content is accepted for French than for Swedish, even though the class distribution in the training data was more skewed toward the negative class for Swedish. This supports our earlier finding that the French source data has a lower ratio of clean text than Swedish (Section 5.1.).

	French	Swedish
Lines	26.89%	29.48%
Words	70.91%	71.47%

Table 10: Proportion of accepted text in Trafilatura output based on mBERT predictions.

5.4. Register annotation results

The register-annotated datasets include 688 documents in French and 1085 in Swedish. The most frequent registers in these datasets as well as the frequencies of the additional flags are show in Tables 11 and 12, and the proportions of the registers in the two languages are illustrated in Figure 3. Although the rankings of the registers differ, the sets of the most frequent registers in the two languages are quite similar. In other words, similar registers seem to be the most frequent ones, and many of the registers described in the annotation scheme (Table 3) remain infrequent. Both languages include a large number of texts labeled as *Description with intent to sell*, *News* and *Personal blog*. Differences arise with *Machine translation, Personal opinion blog* and *Encyclopedia article*. The frequency of *Machine translation* is certainly a sign of its frequency on the Internet. For the other classes, the differences may reflect true language-specific distributions of registers. These will be further examined in future work with more extensive datasets.

Another interesting property in the annotations is that *Informational persuasion* is the only main register among the most frequent ones in both languages. Its frequency may reflect linguistic variation displayed within this register and the fact that documents within it are difficult to assign a specific category. Additionally, it is noteworthy that hybrid categories are relatively infrequent and do not show among the most frequent classes.

The additional flags show the range of linguistic variation and textual composition displayed by the documents. Many of the flags reflect textual properties that can affect the modeling of the documents. *Comments* can be particularly frequent in some registers. In the analyzed data, this is the case with Swedish *Opinion blog* and *Personal blog*. Linguistically, they may be more conversational than the bodies of the texts, which motivates the annotation of the flag.

Similarly, *foreign language* and *generated text* may be used in the text for instance in quotations. These are naturally very different from the language otherwise used in the documents. In our data, *foreign language* seems relatively infrequent, but *generated text* is flagged quite often. Its proportion can, however, decrease when the text cleaning process improves.

Multiple texts and *missing text*, again, are frequent properties of web documents. For instance, a document from a news site may include many headlines and beginnings of the actual news articles, which are then fully displayed on a page of their own. The structuring of these texts may show also in their linguistic characteristics. In our annotation results, these properties are flagged in both languages with frequencies ranging between 0% and 39%. Similar to *comments*, the frequency of these flags can correlate with specific register classes. For instance, 25% of the French and 39% of the Swedish annotations in the *News report* class were flagged as *multiple texts*, while the frequency of this flag was 0% for the *Discussion forum* class in both languages.

Finally, the flag *untypical for the register* reflects linguistic variation within register categories, and is used when the document differs from a typical example of its register. Indicating this helps to further analyze the annotation

	Number of documents	Comments	Missing text	Foreign language	Generated text	Untypical for register	Multiple texts
Description with intent to sell	136	0%	10%	2%	13%	3%	10%
News report / news blog	75	1%	28%	0%	7%	7%	25%
Encyclopedia article	45	0%	18%	0%	22%	7%	2%
Description of a thing	45	0%	16%	2%	20%	0%	2%
Personal blog	33	3%	15%	3%	6%	9%	12%
Discussion forum	33	0%	0%	0%	33%	12%	0%
Reviews	32	3%	16%	0%	28%	9%	22%
How-to / instruction	25	0%	0%	0%	24%	12%	4%
Informational persuasion	25	0%	4%	0%	28%	0%	8%

Table 11: Annotation statistics for the French data

	Number of documents	Comments	Missing text	Foreign language	Generated text	Untypical for register	Multiple texts
Encyclopedia article	223	0%	18%	0%	83%	6%	0.5%
Personal blog	157	32%	8%	6%	31%	2%	9%
Description with intent to sell	136	4%	6%	0%	30%	6%	12%
News report / news blog	109	3%	28%	0%	17%	28%	39%
Opinion blog	45	24%	13%	2%	27%	4%	11%
MT /generated text	37	8%	3%	8%	11%	16%	22%
Description of a thing	27	0%	15%	0%	26%	0%	15%
Discussion forum	20	5%	0%	5%	35%	15%	0%
Informational persuasion	19	0%	11%	0%	32%	0%	16%

Table 12: Annotation statistics for the Swedish data

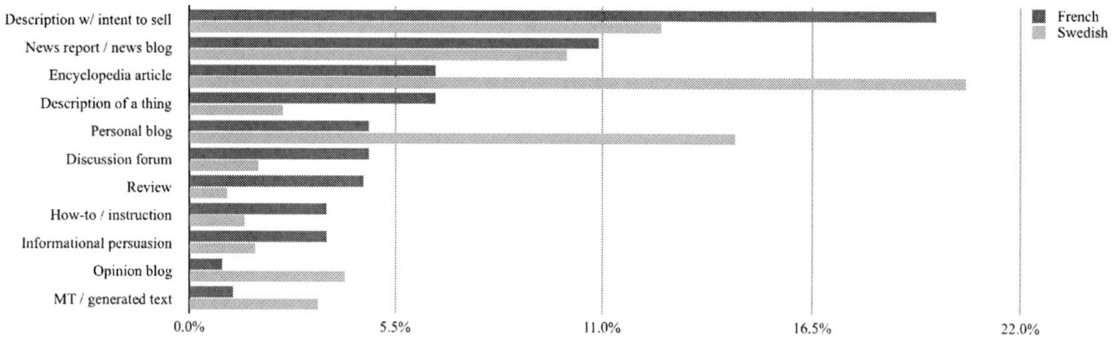

Figure 3: Proportions of registers in the two languages.

decisions if needed. In the annotations, this flag is marked for approximately 10% of the documents. In particular, the flag is frequent in the Swedish *News report* class with a proportion of 28%. This can be symptomatic of the range of linguistic variation within this register.

The register annotation and the different flags are illustrated in Table 13. The example text is annotated as belonging to the Review register. The text is taken from the middle of the original document which is a customer review in an online book store. The actual text is preceded and followed by automatically generated text that is frequent in this kinds of web documents: 'Add to cart' and 'More books on'. The text includes two separate reviews. The first one is present in its entirety, but the second review ends with ... and continues on another page. These properties are described in the annotation by the additional flags.

6. Conclusions and future work

In this study, we have explored the challenges in deriving clean, register-annotated texts from the web. Our starting points were the Swedish and French Common Crawl datasets gathered for the 2017 CoNLL shared task (Ginter et al., 2017), and our approach consisted of three steps: the evaluation of the text quality in order to assess the benefit of boilerplate removal, the development of a classifier to further clean the texts, and the annotation of registers.

First, we manually evaluated three versions of the data that had gone through different cleaning processes: CoNLL versions, raw text versions derived from HTML by stripping markup and cleaned versions extracted from HTML using the boilerplate removal system Trafilatura. The evaluation of the text quality showed that the use of boilerplate removal improves the text quality clearly, although the process also incorrectly rejects some parts belonging to the main text body. In our project, the trade-off – loosing a small proportion of coherent text while improving overall

Original Swedish	Translation
Lägg i varukorg	'Add to cart'
jag tyckte boken var fin med vackra bilder, väntade mig dock mer lantlig känsla, vet ej varför fick bara det intrycket med titeln men alla hem var moderna med stads känsla, inredda med vintage och antikviteter	'i thought the book was nice with beautiful pictures, however, I expected a more rustic feeling, donât know why just got the impression from the title but all the homes were modern with a city-like feeling, decorated with vintage and antiquities '
Vartenda uppslag är fantastiskt! En ren njutning som...	'Every page is fantastic! Pure pleasure that ... '
Fler böcker inom	'More books on'

Table 13: Swedish text example with English translations on the right. Register: Review; Additional flags: Generated text , Part of the text is missing .

quality – is acceptable, as it does not reduce the size of the data substantially.

To facilitate further cleanup of the resulting texts, as a second step, we trained classifiers for distinguishing coherent text content from other, undesirable material. Monolingually fine-tuned Multilingual BERT models achieved the best results for both French and Swedish. Additionally, we tested multi- and cross-lingual settings to investigate to what extent the cleaning could be realized with a joint model or in a language not seen during training. Combining the languages during training in the multilingual setup performed well, but did not outperform the monolingual classifiers. The cross-lingual, zero-shot setting did perform above baseline, which indicates that further cleaning of the texts can be done (to some extent) in multilingual settings without the time-expensive annotation of data in each of the languages under study. This is very encouraging for our project.

Finally, we examined the register annotations and the proportions of different registers in the two languages. This analysis showed that most of the documents belong to a relatively small set of the most frequent registers, although the annotation scheme does cover a wide range of registers and their combinations. Additionally, the sets of the most frequent registers are relatively similar in the two languages. This finding is also very encouraging for our future plans. Specifically, we intend to extend to a larger set of languages already covered in the CoNLL data. We will also experiment with the possibility of combining the line-wise estimates of text quality at the document level. Finally, we will continue the register annotations with the objective of being able to automatically attach detailed register information to all the data.

We release the materials and methods introduced in this study under open licenses at `https://github.com/TurkuNLP/WAC-XII`.

Acknowledgements

The work was funded the Foundation of Emil Aaltonen. Computational resources for this work were provided by CSC – Finnish IT Center for Science.

7. Bibliographical References

Asheghi, N. R., Sharoff, S., and Markert, K. (2016). Crowdsourcing for web genre annotation. *Language Resources and Evaluation*, 50(3):603–641.

Baroni, M., Bernardini, S., Ferraresi, A., and Zanchetta, E. (2009). The wacky wide web: a collection of very large linguistically processed web-crawled corpora. *Language Resources and Evaluation*, 43(3):209–226, September.

Biber, D. and Egbert, J. (2018). *Register variation online*. Cambridge University Press, Cambridge.

Biber, D., Conrad, S., and Reppen, R. (1998). *Corpus Linguistics: Investigating Language Structure and Use*. Cambridge University Press, Cambridge.

Biber, D. (1988). *Variation across speech and writing*. Cambridge University Press, Cambridge.

Bojanowski, P., Grave, E., Joulin, A., and Mikolov, T. (2017). Enriching word vectors with subword information. *Transactions of the Association for Computational Linguistics*, 5:135â146, Dec.

Devlin, J., Chang, M.-W., Lee, K., and Toutanova, K. (2018). BERT: Pre-training of deep bidirectional transformers for language understanding. *arXiv preprint arXiv:1810.04805*.

Egbert, J., Biber, D., and Davies, M. (2015). Developing a bottom-up, user-based method of web register classification. *Journal of the Association for Information Science and Technology*, 66(9):1817–1831.

Ginter, F., Hajič, J., Luotolahti, J., Straka, M., and Zeman, D. (2017). CoNLL 2017 shared task - automatically annotated raw texts and word embeddings. LINDAT/CLARIN digital library at ÚFAL.

Grave, E., Bojanowski, P., Gupta, P., Joulin, A., and Mikolov, T. (2018). Learning word vectors for 157 languages. In *Proceedings of the Eleventh International Conference on Language Resources and Evaluation (LREC 2018)*, Miyazaki, Japan, May. European Language Resources Association (ELRA).

Halliday, M. A. K. (1976). *Cohesion in English*. English language series ; 9. Longman, London.

Joulin, A., Grave, E., Bojanowski, P., and Mikolov, T. (2016). Bag of tricks for efficient text classification. *CoRR*, abs/1607.01759.

Kytö, M. and Ludeling, A. (2008). Collection strategies and design decisions. In *Corpus Linguistics: An International Handbook*, chapter 9.

Laippala, V., Kyllönen, R., Egbert, J., Biber, D., and Pyysalo, S. (2019). Toward multilingual identification of online registers. In *Proceedings of the 22nd Nordic Conference on Computational Linguistics*, pages 292–

297, Turku, Finland, September–October. Linköping University Electronic Press.

McEnery, T. and Wilson, A. (1996). *Corpus Linguistics*. Edinburgh University Press, Edinburgh.

Mikolov, T., Chen, K., Corrado, G., and Dean, J. (2013). Efficient estimation of word representations in vector space. *arXiv preprint arXiv:1301.3781*.

Ortiz Suárez, P. J., Sagot, B., and Romary, L. (2019). Asynchronous Pipeline for Processing Huge Corpora on Medium to Low Resource Infrastructures. In Piotr Bański, et al., editors, *7th Workshop on the Challenges in the Management of Large Corpora (CMLC-7)*, Cardiff, United Kingdom, July. Leibniz-Institut für Deutsche Sprache.

Schäfer, R., Barbaresi, A., and Bildhauer, F. (2013). The good, the bad, and the hazy: Design decisions in web corpus construction. In Stefan Evert, et al., editors, *Proceedings of the 8th Web as Corpus Workshop (WAC-8)*, pages 7–15, Lancaster. SIGWAC.

Schäfer, R. (2016a). Accurate and efficient general-purpose boilerplate detection for crawled web corpora. *Language Resources and Evaluation*. online first.

Schäfer, R. (2016b). Commoncow: Massively huge web corpora from commoncrawl data and a method to distribute them freely under restrictive eu copyright laws. In Nicoletta Calzolari (Conference Chair), et al., editors, *Proceedings of the Tenth International Conference on Language Resources and Evaluation (LREC 2016)*, pages 4500–4504, PortoroÅ$\frac{3}{4}$, Slovenia. European Language Resources Association (ELRA).

Schäfer, R., (2016c). *Proceedings of the 10th Web as Corpus Workshop*, chapter On Bias-free Crawling and Representative Web Corpora, pages 99–105. Association for Computational Linguistics.

Sharoff, S. (2018). Functional text dimensions for the annotation of web corpora. *Corpora*, 1(13):65–95.

Vaswani, A., Shazeer, N., Parmar, N., Uszkoreit, J., Jones, L., Gomez, A. N., Kaiser, Ł., and Polosukhin, I. (2017). Attention is all you need. In *Advances in neural information processing systems*, pages 5998–6008.

Yang, Z., Dai, Z., Yang, Y., Carbonell, J., Salakhutdinov, R., and Le, Q. V. (2019). XLNet: Generalized autoregressive pretraining for language understanding.

Proceedings of the 12th Web as Corpus Workshop, pages 23–32
Language Resources and Evaluation Conference (LREC 2020), Marseille, 11–16 May 2020

Building Web Corpora for Minority Languages

Heidi Jauhiainen, Tommi Jauhiainen, Krister Lindén
University of Helsinki, Department of Digital Humanities
firstname.lastname@helsinki.fi

Abstract

Web corpora creation for minority languages that do not have their own top-level Internet domain is no trivial matter. Web pages in such minority languages often contain text and links to pages in the dominant language of the country. When building corpora in specific languages, one has to decide how and at which stage to make sure the texts gathered are in the desired language. In the "Finno-Ugric Languages and the Internet" (Suki) project, we created web corpora for Uralic minority languages using web crawling combined with a language identification system in order to identify the language while crawling. In addition, we used *language set identification* and crowdsourcing before making sentence corpora out of the downloaded texts. In this article, we describe a strategy for collecting textual material from the Internet for minority languages. The strategy is based on the experiences we gained during the Suki project.

Keywords: web corpora, minority languages, language identification, web-crawling

1. Introduction

Web corpus, as we use the term here, refers to a collection of texts that have been acquired from the World Wide Web and been processed into a static corpus (Fletcher (2012), see also Biemann et al. (2013), Schäfer and Bildhauer (2013)). Making a web text corpus in English is fairly straightforward. If one seeds a web crawler with links to pages written in English, one probably ends up having many texts very quickly. With only a moderate amount of post-processing with existing tools, one can have a corpus in English (Tamura et al., 2007). Finding pages in less dominant languages is more difficult as one has to decide how to effectively find the texts in the desired languages.

Building web corpora in minority languages forms a special case within the corpus creation challenge (Barbaresi, 2015, 127–129). When talking about minority languages in this article, we refer to languages that do not have their own national top-level domain (see e.g. Murphy and Stemle (2011), Schulz et al. (2013)). Searching for texts in national top-level domains is a common way of building corpora in specific languages. However, websites containing minority languages are within the same national domain as those in a majority language, hence some kind of language identification is needed. Pages in minority languages often contain links to pages written in the majority language of the country (Arkhangelskiy, 2019). So, even if one seeds a web crawler with links to pages in the desired language, one quickly ends up with many texts in a majority language.

In this paper, we propose a strategy for building web corpora for minority languages. The strategy is based on our experience with building web corpora for Uralic minority languages in the "Finno-Ugric Languages and the Internet" project[1] (Suki) which was active from 2013 to 2019. The minority languages of the Finno-Ugric language group are used mostly in Northern Europe, Estonia and Russia. The written languages use Latin or Cyrillic alphabets with many special characters. A few of the languages have over half a million speakers, but, for example, Votic only has 11 according to Kuznetsova et al. (2015). The aim of the Suki project was to build web corpora for as many of these minority languages as possible in order to facilitate their survival and revival (Jauhiainen et al., 2015a; Jauhiainen et al., 2019a). In our scope, we included the Samojedic languages (within Russia) which, together with the Finno-Ugric languages, form the larger Uralic language group. We used the *Ethnologue* (Simons and Fennig, 2018) together with the ISO-639-3 standard (SIL, 2013) as our source for the division of Uralic languages. Currently, the *Ethnologue* recognizes 38 different Uralic languages.

We start by reviewing previous work on building language-specific web corpora in Section 2. We then describe the various components we used when gathering sentence corpora, that is, corpora composed of sentences instead of entire texts, for 29 small Uralic languages in Section 3. The lessons we gained from doing this are presented in Section 4. Finally, we introduce the outline of our proposed strategy for building web corpora for minority languages in Section 5. We also provide links to the source code of the technical components that we used in our workflow. All our components are published as open source.

2. Previous Research

The ways in which scholars have tried to find pages for building web corpora in various languages vary. There is also variation in how and at which stage the researchers make sure the pages found are in the desired language. Automatic language identification can be performed using methods ranging from a simple function word checkup to deep neural networks. A recent survey by Jauhiainen et al. (2019d) gives a thorough overview of the subject. In this review of previous research, we concentrate on how the web corpora in specific languages have been obtained.

2.1. Pre-Downloaded Web Collections

Instead of collecting the texts from the Internet directly, it is possible to use pre-downloaded collections. Pomikálek et al. (2012) extracted all pages tagged as English from the

[1] `http://suki.ling.helsinki.fi/eng/project.html`

the Lemur project's[2] ClueWeb09 corpus and then used automatic language identification to make sure the texts used were, in fact, written in English. Common Crawl Foundation[3] regularly crawls the Internet and offers the texts it finds for free download. Smith et al. (2013) downloaded document pairs from the Common Crawl corpus for parallel text corpora of several languages and determined the language of a document using language codes present in the URL. Kanerva et al. (2014) used the morphological analyser OMorFi[4] to find Finnish sentences in the Common Crawl corpus. Using the Common Crawl corpus, Schäfer (2016) built corpora in several languages using the texrex tool[5] while Habernal et al. (2016) built corpora in over 50 languages using a java library to determine the language of a text. Panchenko et al. (2018) built a corpus in English using the C4Corpus tool[6] to find relevant pages in the Common Crawl corpus.

2.2. Search Engines

Several scholars have used automatic creation of search queries to find texts in specific languages on the Internet. Ghani et al. (2001) compiled a script called *Corpus-Builder*,[7] which selects terms from two documents, one relevant and the other not, and constructs a query that uses the conjunction of the terms from the relevant document and the negation of the disjunction of the ones from the non-relevant. The top search engine hit for the query is then downloaded, and the document assigned to either the relevant or non-relevant document set. Search engine queries were also used by Sharoff (2006a) in his corpus building strategy and by Ueyama and Baroni (2005) for building a corpus in Japanese.

Baroni and Bernardini (2004) created a toolkit called *Boot-CaT*,[8] which takes a small set of seed terms and uses queries produced from them to download pages with a search engine. The toolkit was tested by building corpora for English and Italian. BootCaT was also used by Baroni and Ueyama (2004), Sharoff (2006b), and Lyding et al. (2014).

Scannell (2007) built a tool that resembled BootCaT. Depending on the language, the query lists were built with either word lists from a spell checker or word frequency lists. Sometimes language models of trigrams were used to make sure the language was the relevant one. With the tool, Scannell built text corpora for over 400 languages, many of which were under-resourced languages. Arkhangelskiy (2019) used a similar strategy to find texts in seven minority Uralic languages from social media sites. Wagner Filho et al. (2018) also used a toolkit resembling BootCaT called *Web as Corpus Toolkit*[9] for building a web corpus in Brazilian Portuguese.

Schäfer and Bildhauer (2012) recommend that projects wishing to build large web corpora do not use search engine results except as seed URLs for a crawler. The results of their analysis demonstrate that simply downloading the query results with a tool such as BootCaT is not effective enough and that many sites that can be found while crawling the web intensively cannot be found through search engine queries. In addition to this, Sharoff (2006b) and Barbaresi (2013) raise the question of search engines ordering the results according to their "relevance" and the bias this might cause.

2.3. Crawling to Gather Texts

Web crawling is the task of finding large amounts of pages on the web by extracting hyperlinks from already downloaded documents and following them (Olston and Najork, 2010). Web crawlers are used, for example, by search engines to index the web, but also for archiving pages and for data mining. According to Fletcher (2012), it is important to crawl the web if one wants to build web corpora in several languages besides English. Those who have preferred crawling for this have used several different ways of determining what language a page has been written in.

2.3.1. Using URL to Determine a Language

Baykan et al. (2008) wanted to know the language of each page before downloading. They extracted words from URLs and used various machine-learning algorithms to distinguish pages in different languages from each other. Their experiments in various languages showed, however, that English words are prominently present in the URLs of pages in many languages. According to Barbaresi (2013), in case of "lesser-known" languages, language identification of the actual text is necessary even when the words in the URL are used. When searching for pages in Hindi, Priyatam et al. (2012) did prefer to apply a language classifier in addition to the information acquired from the URLs.

2.3.2. Web Page Metadata for Determining Language

The metadata in the HTML source has also been used for determining the language of a page. Somboonviwat et al. (2005) used the information of the pages' charset to determine if they were written in Japanese. Tamura et al. (2007) applied the same method but used TextCat[10] to verify the language of the pages where the charset was found to be UTF-8. They admitted, though, that the metadata check was performed to improve runtime efficiency and that using language identification on pages with other relevant charsets as well would have improved precision.

Identifying the language of a web page by checking the charset in the metadata makes sense only if the language one is interested in uses a special charset. Minority languages are often written using the same encoding as the dominant language of the country they are used in. Furthermore, although many HTML documents contain a language declaration as metadata for the page itself, they are often not used, or used incorrectly (Rehůřek and Kolkus, 2009).

[2] http://www.lemurproject.org/components.php

[3] https://commoncrawl.org

[4] http://flammie.github.io/omorfi/

[5] https://github.com/rsling/texrex

[6] https://dkpro.github.io/dkpro-c4corpus/

[7] http://www.cs.cmu.edu/~TextLearning/corpusbuilder/

[8] https://bootcat.dipintra.it

[9] http://wac-tk.drni.de

[10] https://www.mediawiki.org/wiki/TextCat

2.3.3. Language checking after Crawling

Some scholars have preferred to use some kind of language checking after crawling the web for a corpus. Spoustová and Spousta (2012) and Versley and Panchenko (2012) crawled only some specific, well-chosen sites. Spoustová and Spousta (2012) then used various tools to filter out unwanted texts, whereas Versley and Panchenko (2012) checked the language of each page by inspecting the character encoding and then by using a character trigram-based filter and function words. Emerson and O'Neil (2006) restricted the crawler to accept only pages with metadata language codes indicating the Chinese language. After the crawl, they used the Rosette Language Identifier[11] to detect the language of each page.

Many researchers prefer to crawl national top-level domains where texts in the desired language are believed to be found. Then after the crawl, the language of the pages is verified with various methods. Kornai et al. (2006) applied spell checking to filter out pages that were not in Hungarian. The presence of function words has also been used as a simple form of language identification (Baroni and Kilgariff, 2006; Ferraresi et al., 2008; Baroni et al., 2009), whereas more sophisticated language identifiers were used by Pomikálek et al. (2009) and Schäfer and Bildhauer (2012).

As the .es national domain was very small at the time, Boleda et al. (2006) additionally crawled pages from other domains which were located in Spain in order to build a corpus of Catalan texts. The language of the pages was then identified using a Naive Bayes classifier.

2.3.4. Language Identification during Crawling

Finding web pages dealing with a specific topic is difficult if one just crawls with a standard web crawler (Menczer, 1997; Chakrabarti et al., 1999; Diligenti et al., 2000). A strategy for effectively finding pages on specific topics was proposed by De Bra et al. (1994) and Menczer (1997) but *focused crawling*, an often-used term, was coined by Chakrabarti et al. (1999). A focused crawler assigns a score to the links harvested from a page and the links are handled according to the score they have been assigned thereafter. The idea is that pages on the Internet tend to link to other pages on the same topic (Aggarwal et al., 2001). Somboonviwat et al. (2005) suggested using focused crawling to find pages in specific languages and tested two strategies for doing this. They proposed prioritising links found on pages that had HTML metadata indicating the wanted language and using a threshold for how many irrelevant pages the crawler is allowed to proceed from a relevant one. Schäfer et al. (2014) recommend using the detection of frequent short words and boilerplate to optimise focused web crawling.

In order to prioritise links from a page in a specific language, one needs to check the language while crawling. Many scholars have built web corpora using some kind of focused crawling technique with various language identification methods. Medelyan et al. (2006) used a web crawler named Nutch[12] and identified the language of the pages with TextCat. Mon and Mikami (2011) built their own focused crawler with n-gram based language identification. The links to the subdomain of a page were only added to the outlink queue if the page itself was relevant. Suchomel and Pomikálek (2012) built SpiderLing, a web crawler with inbuilt language models. SpiderLing calculates a yield rate for each page and site. When the yield rate of a site gets too low, it is blacklisted. Barbaresi (2013) used his own crawler to find texts in several different languages and langid.py[13] to identify the language of the crawled pages. He added new links to the download queue only from the relevant pages.

3. Components for building Sentence Corpora for small Uralic Languages

In the Suki project, we started from the premise that crawling the Internet equipped with language identification would give us texts to be processed into corpora in Uralic minority languages. It the end, the main components of our strategy for building web sentence corpora were:

- Acquire the texts using web crawling
- Automatically determine the language using language identification and language set identification
- Verify the automatically identified languages using crowdsourcing
- Tokenise the texts into sentences

3.1. Acquiring texts using web crawling

3.1.1. Choosing a Crawler

Some scholars using web crawlers for collecting pages in specific languages or topics have been concerned that they download too many pages that do not contain what they are looking for (Somboonviwat et al., 2005; Suchomel and Pomikálek, 2012; Schäfer et al., 2014). Schäfer et al. (2014) tried to overcome the problem by collecting seed URLs that were as good quality as possible. Their experiments show that having good-quality seeds is not sufficient when searching for texts in a specific language in national domains containing multiple languages.

Since we were looking for minority languages, we hoped that the relevant pages we found would point to other pages in that language or in other minority languages (Jauhiainen et al., 2019a). We, therefore, needed to do focused crawling and to give precedence to the links found on the pages written in the desired languages. As early as 2006, Boleda et al. (2006) were of the opinion that the technology was advanced enough to do large crawls in order to build web corpora. For such large web crawls, we also needed the crawler to be able to crawl for months if necessary. Obviously, the crawler needed to be polite and respect the general time limits for subsequent downloads from one server as well as the crawl limits and restrictions defined in the robots.txt files of the sites visited (Thelwall and Stuart, 2006; Emerson and O'Neil, 2006).

[11] https://www.basistech.com/text-analytics/rosette/language-identifier/

[12] https://nutch.apache.org

[13] https://github.com/saffsd/langid.py

3.1.2. Heritrix

As our web crawler, we chose Heritrix (Jauhiainen et al., 2015a; Jauhiainen et al., 2019a), a web archiving system developed by the Internet Archive (Mohr et al. (2004), see also Emerson and O'Neil (2006)).[14] Heritrix is used by several national libraries around the world to collect national web archives and it has been successfully used to collect text corpora by Baroni and Kilgariff (2006), Emerson and O'Neil (2006), Ferraresi et al. (2008), Baroni et al. (2009), Pomikálek et al. (2009), Schäfer and Bildhauer (2012) and Versley and Panchenko (2012). Heritrix obeys the robots.txt exclusion directives and has a system for giving precedence to specific links. Heritrix is open source and extendable, so we were also able to make custom changes to it.

3.1.3. Scope

When dealing with minority languages, the researchers usually have an idea which domains texts in the relevant languages could possibly be found in. We started collecting texts in Uralic minority languages by crawling, one by one, the .ee, .fi, .hu, .lv, .no, .ru, and .se domains (Jauhiainen et al., 2019a). According to Schäfer and Bildhauer (2013), large seed lists are only needed if one wants to find relevant pages as quickly as possible. Since we were crawling for minority pages anywhere in the national domains and hence were conducting large, long-lasting crawls, we seeded them with links to the home pages of the universities in these countries. We hoped that these sites with many outlinks would allow us to have very broad crawls in the long run. The university pages might also contain links from research projects to sites in small Uralic languages.

As we were building corpora from the texts found on the Internet, we were not interested in the links pointing to files not containing natural language, such as pictures (Jauhiainen et al., 2015a; Jauhiainen et al., 2019a). Such a strategy of ignoring the media files was also used for web corpus building by, for example, Baroni and Kilgariff (2006) and Ferraresi et al. (2008). After intensive testing with large crawls, we ended up using 600 threads at once, crawling only up to 20 links away from the seeds (in order to avoid, for example, getting stuck in a calendar or an online shop) and retiring download queues after they reached 100,000 links (as some sites may be replicating pages).

We conducted one-month long crawls for each of the national domains we were interested in. After one month of crawling, the number of queues was already quite low and the average speed had gone from about 300 URLs per second down to under 5 (under 100 in the .ru domain). Later, we conducted a two-month crawl which, in addition to all the relevant national domains, included the .com domain. This crawl was seeded with the URLs of the relevant pages found in the previous crawls.

3.2. Automatic Language Identification

3.2.1. Improving Language Identification

Part of the Suki project was dedicated to improving the state-of-the-art of language identification in texts and we further developed the language identification method by Jauhiainen (2010). Our language identifiers have fared very well in several shared tasks dedicated to distinguishing between close languages (Jauhiainen et al., 2018a; Jauhiainen et al., 2018b; Jauhiainen et al., 2019c). For collecting corpora in minority languages, we used an implementation of the HeLI method (Jauhiainen et al., 2016), based on which we created a language identifier service[15] that takes in text and responds with a corresponding language code. Currently the language identifier in production can distinguish between c. 400 languages and dialects in out-of-domain contexts (Jauhiainen et al., 2017). At the beginning of the project, we were able to find suitable training material for 34 of the 38 Uralic languages (Jauhiainen et al., 2015a; Jauhiainen et al., 2019a).[16] Hungarian, Finnish, and Estonian were not relevant as they are majority languages and thus we had 31 Uralic minority languages.

3.2.2. Language Identification While Crawling

In order to use language identification while crawling, we made some custom changes to the code of Heritrix. After downloading a file, we stripped the text of all the HTML markup before it was sent to the language identifier service. Our initial idea was to identify the text of the whole page, but in doing so we quickly encountered problems with speed. Identifying the whole page took too long when it was done while crawling. The crawler was able to process up to 400 pages per second and we needed the language identifier service to be able to keep up with that speed. We solved the problem by taking three excerpts of 100 characters from the entire text. Pages with fewer than 300 characters were ignored. The excerpts were sent as one package to the language identifier service where each was identified separately (Jauhiainen et al., 2015a; Jauhiainen et al., 2019a). If even one of the excerpts was identified as having been written in one of the languages of interest, the whole text of the page was sent to be identified. If the text of the entire page was still identified as one of the small Uralic languages, the text of the page was archived. The links found on such pages were given precedence over links from other pages in the frontier queue of the crawler (Jauhiainen et al., 2015a; Jauhiainen et al., 2019a).

3.3. Language Set Identification

The texts of web pages are often multilingual (Kilgarriff and Grefenstette, 2003), especially those including minority languages (Boleda et al., 2006). Most language identification methods are, however, built for identifying the language of a monolingual text (Lui et al., 2014; Jauhiainen et al., 2015b). When a monolingual language identifier is used to identify the language of a text written in multiple languages, it might, depending on the algorithm, produce an answer unrelated to the actual languages within the text (Prager, 1999). In the Suki project, we encountered this problem in practice when we were manually verifying the languages of the web pages automatically identified to be relevant. With language set identification, we refer to the

[14] `http://www.archive.org`

[15] `https://github.com/tosaja/TunnistinPalveluFast`

[16] No digitally encoded texts were found for Akkala, Ter, and Pite Saami languages nor for the Kamas language.

task of determining which languages are present in a document or text segment (Lui et al., 2014; Jauhiainen et al., 2015b).

3.3.1. The Method

Even though multilingual language identification for corpora creation purposes had been studied previously (Ludovik and Zacharski, 1999), there was no suitable off-the-shelf multilingual language identifier for us to use. For our project, we developed a new language set identification method (Jauhiainen et al., 2015b) which we named MultiLI.[17] The method uses a fixed size character window and, as the window slides stepwise along a text, the text of each window is identified with a language identifier. The language of the first window is stored in a variable called "current language" and when the language of subsequent windows has been different from the "current language" variable more times than a threshold, the language of the variable is changed. The method keeps track of all the languages that have been the "current language" at some point and returns these languages as a list.

3.3.2. Post-Crawl Language Set Identification

After the crawls of the national domains and the .com domain, all the texts found to possibly contain relevant languages were re-processed with MultiLI. Using the language set identifier, we could more easily find the pages containing any of the target languages (Jauhiainen et al., 2019a).
In addition to a list of languages, MultiLI provides the approximate percentages of those languages in the text of the whole page. As we did not want to miss any pages containing even a small amount of text in a relevant Uralic language, we accepted all texts of which at least 2% was in one of them.
One important function that MultiLI provided at this stage was the unknown language or "junk" detection. By not accepting any pages that were identified to have more than 9 languages, we did get rid of many pages that did not contain proper text at all.
We also downloaded the Common Crawl archive from December 2014.[18] We first used HeLI to identify the languages of the almost two billion pages in the archive. We then performed a more precise analysis with MultiLI on the 155,000 texts that had been identified by HeLI as having been written in a Uralic minority language. In this way, we found many new relevant links outside the national domains we had crawled ourselves (Jauhiainen et al., 2019a).

3.4. Crowdsourcing

There is a limit to how accurate automatic language identification can be. The accuracy of the identifier depends on the similarity of the training data to the texts that the crawler encounters in the wild. Even though the number of languages known by the language identifier can be high, it will almost certainly encounter languages it does not know. It will also encounter non-lingual or multilingual texts that can resemble one or more of the relevant languages (Schäfer and Bildhauer, 2013, 58). It is also possible that one of the relevant languages can be encountered which is written using a previously unknown orthography or is simply from a completely different domain than the material used for training, both of which prevent us from tightening the precision of the identifier too much.
As we ourselves were not familiar with most of the small Uralic languages, we planned to outsource the language verification to native speakers and linguists using crowdsourcing. One of the goals of the Suki project was to create a portal page with links to web pages that had been written in the relevant languages. We included the necessary crowdsourcing functionality into the portal site, which we call Wanca.[19] We were and are still not aware of similar platforms available for this purpose, which led us to develop our own.[20]
After removing exact duplicates, we uploaded to Wanca all the URLs of the texts that were still thought relevant after language set identification (Jauhiainen et al., 2019a). The URLs were accompanied by the language tag given by MultiLI as the most prominent relevant language for each page.
In Wanca, registered users can vote for or against the language currently assigned to a page. The native speakers and linguists were advised to try to determine the largest relevant language for each page. A user with "expert user" rights is also allowed to verify the current language, which removes the voting option from the platform. An "expert user" could also change the current language to another, thus verifying the new language. The operations of verifying and changing the language could also be done to a whole website at once.
Originally we had published almost half a million links in Wanca. Since 2015, many automatically identified languages have been verified and, more importantly, almost 200,000 links that turned out not to be relevant have been discarded by us or the other users of the Wanca platform. By the time of the writing, Wanca contains 288,799 links that are considered to have been written in a Uralic minority language.

3.5. Sentence corpora pipeline

Since we do not automatically have copyrights for the downloaded texts (Fletcher, 2012; Schäfer, 2016), our aim was to create sentence corpora under the assumption that one sentence out of context can very rarely be considered to have individual copyright (Fletcher, 2012). We have described the sentence corpora creation pipeline in detail in an earlier article (Jauhiainen et al., 2019a).[21] In short, we started with the URLs tagged with relevant languages in Wanca and re-ran the corresponding texts through the language set identifier MultiLI. This time we carried the language set information forward and used it later to narrow

[17] `https://github.com/tosaja/TunnistinPalveluMulti`
[18] `http://commoncrawl.org/2015/01/december-2014-crawl-archive-available/`
[19] `http://suki.ling.helsinki.fi/wanca/`
[20] `https://github.com/uhdigihum/WancaPlatform`
[21] `https://github.com/uhdigihum/SUKISentencePipeline`

down the repertoire of languages available for the identifier. We divided the texts into individual lines keeping only those that our sentence tokeniser would later be able to find sentences from. We processed each line using the language set identifier and allowed the identifier only to indicate those relevant languages that were indicated in the set of the whole page. Each line was then split into sentences using a sentence tokenisation algorithm common to the languages involved (Jauhiainen et al., 2019a) using abbreviation guessing heuristics presented by (Mikheev, 2002). Afterwards, the language of each individual sentence was identified using MultiLI and the most prominent language indicated by it was set as the language of the sentence. We removed duplicate sentences as the Internet is full of web services that automatically generate text in natural languages, and the duplicate sentences probably do not represent any natural frequency used by humans. Finally, sentences written in relevant languages were added to corresponding sentence collections.

3.6. Corpora

From time to time, we have re-crawled the links that are considered relevant to see if the pages still exist. Since we first crawled for texts in Uralic minority languages, 80% of the links and 90% of the sites we found have either disappeared or their robots.txt directives have been tightened. To create the sentence corpora, we used a re-crawl from 2016 where we had texts from 119,052 pages. After our pipeline, we ended up with 646,043 unique sentences in 29 languages. The sentences come from 39,731 pages. The sentence corpora created in the Suki project were published at the Language Bank of Finland in their Korp service in 2019.[22] A downloadable version of the corpora was made available in the spring of 2020.[23]

4. Lessons learned

We only created our sentence corpora pipeline after the languages of the pages had been curated in Wanca by us and the language experts. The amount of junk and texts in unknown languages was considerable. In the beginning, we discarded complete sites as junk as the sources for language identification errors were apparent after inspecting only a few pages within a site. Many of the errors were in the parts of the texts which did not contain complete sentences, but were, for example, lists of the names of mechanical components. This is why we suggest using the sentence creation pipeline even before uploading the URLs to a crowdsourcing platform. Only those pages where at least one proper sentence is written in one of the relevant languages should be forwarded to manual inspection. This would probably get rid of much junk and irrelevant pages without anyone having to go through them manually. It is important that the native speakers and linguists donating their time and skills feel that their work is valuable and meaningful.

The parameters of the language identifier must be adjusted so that it is able to keep up with the speed of the crawler. When the HeLI method uses a very large word and character n-gram vocabulary it is slow to start. However, when it is offered as a service and the models are already loaded in memory, the size of the models does not essentially affect the speed of the identification process. The number of languages available to the identifier, however, has an impact on the identification speed linear to the number of languages.

The number and size of the excerpts sent to the language identifier while crawling must be decided, taking into account the capabilities of the hardware used. We used three short excerpts, but if the hardware allows, more excerpts can be tested. If the relevant languages can be identified with sufficient recall using shorter segments, then more of these shorter excerpts could be used. Thus, the length of each excerpt is determined by the accuracy of the language identifier used. As a shorter segment of text is less likely to contain several languages, using shorter excerpts also helps in dealing with multilingual pages.

When one is targeting minority languages, one does not want to miss any potential texts while crawling, hence errors in precision are much more acceptable than errors in recall. In hindsight, if the three excerpts contained a relevant language, re-identifying the language of the whole text while crawling was a mistake. The later stages of our process would have removed the incorrectly identified texts, but since we relied on the identification of the language of the whole text, we may have missed some multilingual ones.

The HeLI method is very fast and precise when dealing with languages that can be separated into words easily by, for example, using whitespaces as delimiters. In case the relevant languages include ones that do not use whitespaces, we suggest employing other methods. For example, we used Naive Bayes in our winning submission to the track for traditional Chinese of the Discriminating between the Mainland and Taiwan variation of Mandarin Chinese (DMT) shared task (Jauhiainen et al., 2019c).

One reason why we have not been eager to publish the language models of the service in production together with our code is the fact that we have only been improving the recall and precision of the languages relevant to the Suki project. As the source texts for other language models were mostly gathered from Wikipedia, some of these models, for example English, have severe problems with recall and precision. Another reason is that the complete models used in production with the crawler take in total 20 gigabytes of space and it is not trivial to distribute files of this size. It is future work to prune or optimise the data structure without losing identification speed or accuracy.

5. Proposed strategy

In this section, we introduce the strategy that we recommend for web sentence corpora creation for minority languages based on our trials and documented experience. First, we present the suggested stages of the web corpora building strategy. Second, we list the technical components that can be used to implement the strategy.

5.1. Strategy outline

Stage 1. Decide which top-level Internet domains are relevant to your crawl. Gather a list of prominent websites for each top-level domain to use as seeds for each crawl.

[22] `http://urn.fi/urn:nbn:fi:lb-2019052401`
[23] `http://urn.fi/urn:nbn:fi:lb-2020022901`

If you already know of websites written in the language of interest, use them as seeds as well.

Stage 2. Start a breadth-first crawl within the given domain and identify the possible languages of each page by taking as many extracts from the page as is possible given the speed of your language identifier service. Use a language identifier optimised for recall of the relevant languages, as you do not want to miss any possible sources at this point. Precision for the relevant languages can be sacrificed if more speed is needed. If even one extract is indicated to be written in a relevant language, store the whole text.

Stage 3. After the crawl, remove duplicate or near-duplicate texts. We suggest removing duplicates that differ from each other only by non-alphabetic (or non-logographic) characters, for example by different timestamps.

Stage 4. Process all the stored texts using a language set identifier. If too many languages are detected for one file it is probably written in a language unknown to the language identifier or contains large amounts of non-lingual material, such as lists of product codes. If the set of identified languages is reasonable, keep texts that include at least one language relevant to your corpus. Store the language set and the URL as text-specific metadata.

Stage 5. Segment the texts into sentences and retain only complete sentences. If your sentence tokeniser cannot span line-breaks, you can first use the language set identifier to identify each line and keep only those in the relevant languages.

Stage 6. Identify the language of each sentence using only the relevant languages indicated by the previous level language set identification. Tag each sentence with the majority language indicated by the language set identifier.

Stage 7. Retain only those texts that include at least one sentence in a relevant language. Tag the retained texts with the relevant language in which the most sentences are written.

Stage 8. Use experts and native speakers to verify that the retained pages actually include relevant languages. In case some of the pages have been removed from the Internet, but the text had duplicates or near-duplicates, use the first working address from the duplicate list. Remove those texts that are clearly rejected by crowdsourcing.

Stage 9. In case you have special language-dependent sentence tokenisers for the relevant languages, you might want to re-tokenise the original text at this stage and then remove duplicate sentences within the same language. Otherwise, use the sentences and their identifications generated at stages 5 and 6.

Stage 10. Shuffle the sentences and add them to their language-specific collections.

5.2. Technical components

Web crawling To collect the texts for our "Wanca in Korp 2016" corpus (Jauhiainen et al., 2019b), we used Heritrix version 3.1. Currently, we have an operational version of Heritrix 3.3. The modified version of Heritrix 3.3 containing the enhanced text pre-processing and the ability to use a language identifier service is available on GitHub.[24]

Language identification We have published the monolingual language identifier service implementing the HeLI algorithm on GitHub.[25] While preparing this article, we improved the documentation and included character *n*-gram models from one to six characters as well as individual words for Finnish and Swedish as an example.

Language set identification The language set identifier MultiLI, which uses HeLI together with the language set identification algorithm is also available on GitHub.[26] It does not contain any language models, but it can use the same language models as the monolingual language identifier service.

Crowdsourcing platform The code for the Wanca platform is also available on GitHub.[27]

Sentence tokeniser The sentence tokeniser and the scripts for the whole sentence corpora pipeline are available on GitHub.[28]

6. Conclusions

We have presented the strategy we used to create sentence corpora for Uralic minority languages, analysed its usability, and suggested an improved version of the strategy. We believe that the strategy could be used to build web corpora for other minority languages that have web pages in the same national top-level domain as the majority language of the country or countries in which the languages are used. Building web corpora for minority languages is an important undertaking for the preservation of these under-resourced and often endangered languages. The crowdsourcing platform can be used to inform the native language users of the resources available online.

7. Acknowledgements

This work has been funded by the Kone Foundation, the Academy of Finland, and FIN-CLARIN. The authors would like to thank all those users of the Wanca platform who have contributed to the language verifying effort as well as the anonymous reviewers of this article for their valuable comments.

8. Bibliographical References

Aggarwal, C. C., Al-Garawi, F., and Yu, P. S. (2001). Intelligent Crawling on the World Wide Web with Arbitrary Predicates. In *Proceedings of the 10th International Conference on World Wide Web (WWW '01)*, pages 96–105, New York, NY, USA. ACM.

Arkhangelskiy, T. (2019). Corpora of social media in minority Uralic languages. In *of the Fifth International Workshop on Computational Linguistics for Uralic Languages (IWCLUL 2019)*, pages 125–140, Tartu, Estonia.

[24] https://github.com/uhdigihum/heritrix3

[25] https://github.com/tosaja/TunnistinPalveluFast

[26] https://github.com/tosaja/TunnistinPalveluMulti

[27] https://github.com/uhdigihum/WancaPlatform

[28] https://github.com/uhdigihum/SUKISentencePipeline

Barbaresi, A. (2013). Crawling microblogging services to gather language-classified URLs: Workflow and case study. In *Proceedings of the Student Research Workshop (ACL 2013)*, pages 9–15, Sofia, Bulgaria.

Barbaresi, A. (2015). *Ad hoc and general-purpose corpus construction from web sources*. Ph.D. thesis, École Normale Supérieure de Lyon.

Baroni, M. and Bernardini, S. (2004). BootCaT: Bootstrapping Corpora and Terms from the Web. In *Proceedings of the International Conference on Language Resources and Evaluation (LREC 2004)*, Lisbon, Portugal.

Baroni, M. and Kilgariff, A. (2006). Large linguistically-processed Web corpora for multiple languages. In *Proceedings of the 11th Conference of the European Chapter of the Association for Computational Linguistics (EACL 2006)*, pages 87–90, Trento, Italy.

Baroni, M. and Ueyama, M. (2004). Retrieving Japanese specialized terms and corpora from the World Wide Web. In *Proceedings of the 7th Conference on Natural Language Processing (KONVENS 2004)*, Wien, Austria.

Baroni, M., Bernardini, S., Ferraresi, A., and Zanchetta, E. (2009). The WaCky wide web: a collection of very large linguistically processed web-crawled corpora. *Language Resources and Evaluation*, 43(3):209–226.

Baykan, E., Henzinger, M., and Weber, I. (2008). Web Page Language Identification Based on URLs. In *Proceedings of the 34th International Conference on Very Large Data Bases (VLDB '08)*, pages 176–187, Auckland, New Zealand.

Biemann, C., Bildhauer, F., Evert, S., Goldhahn, D., Quasthoff, U., Schäfer, R., Simon, J., Swiezinski, L., and Zesch, T. (2013). Scalable Construction of High-Quality Web Corpora. *JLCL*, 28:23–59.

Boleda, G., Bott, S., Meza, R., Castillo, C., Badia, T., and Lopez, V. (2006). CUCWeb: a Catalan corpus built from the Web. In *Proceedings of the 2nd International Workshop on Web as Corpus (WAC '06)*, pages 19–26, Trento, Italy.

Chakrabarti, S., Van den Berg, M., and Dom, B. (1999). Focused crawling: a new approach to topic-specific Web resource discovery. *Computer Networks*, 31(11):1623–1640.

De Bra, P., Houben, G.-J., Kornatzky, Y., and Post, R. (1994). Information Retrieval in Distributed Hypertexts. In *Proceeding of Computer-Assisted Information Retrieval (RIAO 1994)*, pages 481–491, NY, NY.

Diligenti, M., Coetzee, F. M., Lawrence, S., Giles, C. L., and Gori, M. (2000). Focused crawling Using Context Graphs. In *Proceedings of the 26th International Conference on Very Large Data Bases (VLDB 2000)*, pages 527–534, Cairo, Egypt.

Emerson, T. and O'Neil, J. (2006). Experience Building a Large Corpus for Chinese Lexicon Construction. In Marco Baroni et al., editors, *WaCky! Working papers on the Web as Corpus*, pages 41–62. Bologna: GEDIT.

Ferraresi, A., Zanchetta, E., Baroni, M., and Bernardini, S. (2008). Introducing and evaluating ukWaC, a very large web-derived corpus of English. In *Proceedings of the 4th International Workshop on Web as Corpus (WAC-4)*, pages 47–54, Marrakech, Morocco.

Fletcher, W. H. (2012). Corpus Analysis of the World Wide Web. In C.A. Chapelle, editor, *The Encyclopedia of Applied Linguistics*. American Cancer Society.

Ghani, R., Jones, R., and Mladenič, D. (2001). Mining the Web to Create Minority Language Corpora. In *Proceedings of the 10th International Conference on Information and Knowledge Management (ACM CIKM 2001)*, pages 279–286, Atlanta, Georgia.

Habernal, I., Zayed, O., and Gurevych, I. (2016). C4Corpus: Multilingual Web-size Corpus with Free License. In Nicoletta Calzolari, et al., editors, *Proceedings of the 10th International Conference on Language Resources and Evaluation (LREC 2016)*, Paris, France.

Jauhiainen, H., Jauhiainen, T., and Lindén, K. (2015a). The Finno-Ugric Languages and The Internet Project. In *Proceedings of the 1st International Workshop on Computational Linguistics for Uralic Languages (IWCLUL 2015)*, number 2 in Septentrio Conference Series, pages 87–98.

Jauhiainen, T., Lindén, K., and Jauhiainen, H. (2015b). Language Set Identification in Noisy Synthetic Multilingual Documents. In A. Gelbukh, editor, *Proceedings of the Computational Linguistics and Intelligent Text Processing 16th International Conference, (CICLing 2015)*, Part I of Lecture Notes in Computer Science, pages 633–643, Cairo, Egypt. Springer.

Jauhiainen, T., Lindén, K., and Jauhiainen, H. (2016). HeLI, a Word-Based Backoff Method for Language Identification. In *Proceedings of the 3rd Workshop on NLP for Similar Languages, Varieties and Dialects (VarDial 2016)*, pages 153–162, Osaka, Japan.

Jauhiainen, T., Lindén, K., and Jauhiainen, H. (2017). Evaluation of Language Identification Methods Using 285 Languages. In *Proceedings of the 21st Nordic Conference on Computational Linguistics (NoDaLiDa 2017)*, pages 183–191, Gothenburg, Sweden.

Jauhiainen, T., Jauhiainen, H., and Lindén, K. (2018a). HeLI-based experiments in Swiss German dialect identification. In *Proceedings of the 5th Workshop on NLP for Similar Languages, Varieties and Dialects (VarDial 2018)*, pages 254–262, Santa Fe, New Mexico.

Jauhiainen, T., Jauhiainen, H., and Lindén, K. (2018b). Iterative Language Model Adaptation for Indo-Aryan Language Identification. In *Proceedings of the 5th Workshop on NLP for Similar Languages, Varieties and Dialects (VarDial 2018)*, pages 66–75, Santa Fe, New Mexico.

Jauhiainen, H., Jauhiainen, T., and Linden, K. (2019a). Wanca in Korp: Text corpora for underresourced Uralic languages. In Jarmo Harri Jantunen, et al., editors, *Proceedings of the Research data and humanities (RDHUM) 2019 conference*, number 17 in Studia Humaniora Ouluensia, pages 21–40, Finland. University of Oulu.

Jauhiainen, H., Jauhiainen, T., and Lindén, K. (2019b). Wanca 2016, Korp Version (BETA). [text corpus]. Kielipankki. Retrieved from http://urn.fi/urn:nbn:fi:lb-2019052401.

Jauhiainen, T., Jauhiainen, H., and Lindén, K. (2019c).

Discriminating between Mandarin Chinese and Swiss-German varieties using adaptive language models. In *Proceedings of the 6th Workshop on NLP for Similar Languages, Varieties and Dialects (VarDial 2019)*, pages 178–187, Minneapolis, Minnesota.

Jauhiainen, T., Lui, M., Zampieri, M., Baldwin, T., and Lindén, K. (2019d). Automatic Language Identification in Texts: A Survey. *Journal of Artificial Intelligence Research*, 65:675–782.

Jauhiainen, T. (2010). Tekstin kielen automaattinen tunnistaminen. Master's thesis, University of Helsinki, Helsinki.

Kanerva, J., Luotolahti, J., Laippala, V., and Ginter, F. (2014). Syntactic N-gram Collection from a Large-Scale Corpus of Internet Finnish. In Andrius Utka, et al., editors, *Proceedings of the Sixth International Conference Baltic HLT 2014*, volume 268 of *Frontiers in Artificial Intelligence and Applications*, pages 184–191.

Kilgarriff, A. and Grefenstette, G. (2003). Web as Corpus. *Computational Linguistics*, 29(3):333–347.

Kornai, A., Halácsy, P., Nagy, V., Oravecz, C., Trón, V., and Varga, D. (2006). Web-based frequency dictionaries for medium density languages. In *Proceedings of the 2nd International Workshop on Web as Corpus (WAC '06)*, Trento, Italy.

Kuznetsova, N., Markus, E., and Muslimov, M. (2015). Finnic Minorities of Ingria. In Heiko F. Marten, et al., editors, *Cultural and Linguistic Minorities in the Russian Federation and the European Union: Comparative Studies on Equality and Diversity*, pages 127–167. Springer.

Ludovik, Y. and Zacharski, R. (1999). Multilingual Document Language Recognition for Creating Corpora. Technical report, New Mexico State University.

Lui, M., Lau, J. H., and Baldwin, T. (2014). Automatic Detection and Language Identification of Multilingual Documents. *Transactions of the Association for Computational Linguistics*, 2:27–40.

Lyding, V., Stemle, E., Borghetti, C., Brunello, M., Castagnoli, S., Dell'Orletta, F., Dittmann, H., Lenci, A., and Pirrelli, V. (2014). The PAISÀ Corpus of Italian Web Texts. In *Proceedings of the 9th International Workshop on Web as Corpus (WaC-9)*, pages 36–43, Gothenburg, Sweden.

Medelyan, O., Schulz, S., Paetzold, J., Poprat, M., and Marcó, K. (2006). Language Specific and Topic Focused Web Crawling. In *Proceedings of the 5th International Conference on Language Resources and Evaluation (LREC'06)*, pages 865–868, Genoa, Italy.

Menczer, F. (1997). ARACHNID: Adaptive Retrieval Agents Choosing Heuristic Neighborhoods. In *Proceedings of the 14th International Conference on Machine Learning*, pages 227–235.

Mikheev, A. (2002). Periods, Capitalized Words, etc. *Computational Linguistics*, 28(13):289–318.

Mohr, G., Stack, M., Rnitovic, I., Avery, D., and Kimpton, M. (2004). Introduction to Heritrix. 4th International Web Archiving Workshop (at ECDL2004).

Mon, P. Y. and Mikami, Y. (2011). Myanmar Language Search Engine. *International Journal of Computer Science Issues (IJCSI)*, 8(2):118–126.

Murphy, B. and Stemle, E. W. (2011). PaddyWaC: A minimally-supervised web-corpus of hiberno-English. In *Proceedings of the 1st Workshop on Algorithms and Resources for Modelling of Dialects and Language Varieties*, pages 22–29, Edinburgh, Scotland. Association for Computational Linguistics.

Olston, C. and Najork, M. (2010). Web Crawling. *Foundations and Trends in Information Retrieval*, 4(3):175–246.

Panchenko, A., Ruppert, E., Faralli, S., Ponzetto, S. P., and Biemann, C. (2018). Building a Web-Scale Dependency-Parsed Corpus from CommonCrawl. In Nicoletta Calzolari, et al., editors, *Proceedings of the 11th International Conference on Language Resources and Evaluation (LREC 2018)*, Miyazaki, Japan.

Pomikálek, J., Rychlý, P., and Kilgarriff, A. (2009). Scaling to Billion-plus Word Corpora. *Advances in Computational Linguistics*, 41(3):3–13.

Pomikálek, J., Jakubícek, M., and Rychlỳ, P. (2012). Building a 70 billion word corpus of English from ClueWeb. In *Proceedings of the 8th International Conference on Language Resources and Evaluation (LREC 2012)*, pages 502–506, Istanbul, Turkey.

Prager, J. M. (1999). Linguini: Language Identification for Multilingual Documents. In *Proceedings of the 32nd Annual Hawaii International Conference on Systems Sciences (HICSS-32)*, Maui, Hawaii.

Priyatam, P. N., Vaddepally, S., and Varma, V. (2012). Domain Specific Search in Indian Languages. In *Proceedings of the 1st workshop on Information and knowledge management for developing regions (IKM4DR'12)*, pages 23–30, Maui, Hawaii.

Rehůřek, R. and Kolkus, M. (2009). Language Identification on the Web: Extending the Dictionary Method. In A. Gelbukh, editor, *Proceedings of the Computational Linguistics and Intelligent Text Processing 10th International Conference, (CICLing 2009)*, Lecture Notes in Computer Science, pages 357–368, Mexico City, Mexico. Springer.

Scannell, K. P. (2007). The Crúbadán Project: Corpus building for under-resourced languages. *Cahiers du Cental*, 5(1):1–10.

Schulz, S., Lyding, V., and Nicolas, L. (2013). Compiling a diverse web corpus for South Tyrolean German - STirWaC. In Stefan Evert, et al., editors, *Proceedings of the 8th Web as Corpus Workshop (WAC-8)*, pages 37–45.

Schäfer, R. and Bildhauer, F. (2012). Building large corpora from the web using a new efficient tool chain. In *Proceedings of the 8th International Conference on Language Resources and Evaluation (LREC'12)*, Istanbul, Turkey.

Schäfer, R. and Bildhauer, F. (2013). *Web Corpus Construction*. Synthesis Lectures on Human Language Technologies. Morgan and Claypool, San Francisco.

Schäfer, R., Barbaresi, A., and Bildhauer, F. (2014). Focused Web Corpus Crawling. In *Proceedings of the 9th International Workshop on Web as Corpus (WaC-9)*, pages 9–15, Gothenburg, Sweden.

Schäfer, R. (2016). CommonCOW: Massively Huge Web Corpora from CommonCrawl Data and a Method to Distribute them Freely under Restrictive EU Copyright Laws. In Nicoletta Calzolari, et al., editors, *Proceedings of the 10th International Conference on Language Resources and Evaluation (LREC 2016)*, Paris, France.

Sharoff, S. (2006a). Open-source Corpora: using the net to fish for linguistic data. *International Journal of Corpus Linguistics*, 11(4):435–462.

Sharoff, S. (2006b). Creating general-purpose corpora using automated search engine queries. In Marco Baroni et al., editors, *WaCky! Working papers on the Web as Corpus*, pages 63–98. Bologna: GEDIT.

SIL. (2013). *ISO 639-3 Codes for the representation of names of languages*. SIL International.

Gary F. Simons et al., editors. (2018). *Ethnologue: Languages of the World, Twenty-first edition*. SIL International, Dallas, Texas.

Smith, J. R., Saint-Amand, H., Plamada, M., Koehn, P., Callison-Burch, C., and Lopez, A. (2013). Dirt Cheap Web-Scale Parallel Text from the Common Crawl. In *Proceedings of the 51st Annual Meeting of the Association for Computational Linguistics (Volume 1: Long Papers)*, pages 1374–1383, Sofia, Bulgaria.

Somboonviwat, K., Tamura, T., and Kitsuregawa, M. (2005). Simulation Study of Language Specific Web Crawling. In *Proceedings of the 21st International Conference on Data Engineering Workshops (ICDEW'05)*, Tokyo, Japan.

Spoustová, J. and Spousta, M. (2012). A High-Quality Web Corpus of Czech. In *Proceedings of the 8th International Conference on Language Resources and Evaluation (LREC'12)*, pages 311–315, Istanbul, Turkey.

Suchomel, V. and Pomikálek, J. (2012). Efficient Web Crawling for Large Text Corpora. In *Proceedings of the 7th International Workshop on Web as Corpus (WAC-7)*, pages 39–43, Lyon, France.

Tamura, T., Somboonviwat, K., and Kitsuregawa, M. (2007). A Method for Language-Specific Web Crawling and Its Evaluation. *Systems and Computers in Japan*, 38(2):10–20.

Thelwall, M. and Stuart, D. (2006). Web Crawling Ethics Revisited: Cost, Privacy, and Denial of Service. *Journal of the American Society for Information Science and Technology*, 57(13):1771–1779.

Ueyama, M. and Baroni, M. (2005). Automated construction and evaluation of Japanese Web-based reference corpora. In *Proceedings of 3th Corpus Linguistics Conference*, Birmingham, United Kingdom.

Versley, Y. and Panchenko, Y. (2012). Not Just Bigger: Towards Better-Quality Web Corpora. In *Proceedings of the 7th International Workshop on Web as Corpus (WAC-7)*, pages 45–52.

Wagner Filho, J. A., Wilkens, R., Idiart, M., and Villavicencio, A. (2018). The brWaC Corpus: A New Open Resource for Brazilian Portuguese. In Nicoletta Calzolari, et al., editors, *Proceedings of the Eleventh International Conference on Language Resources and Evaluation (LREC 2018)*, Miyazaki, Japan.

Proceedings of the 12th Web as Corpus Workshop, pages 33–41
Language Resources and Evaluation Conference (LREC 2020), Marseille, 11–16 May 2020

The `ELTE.DH Pilot Corpus` – Creating a Handcrafted Gigaword Web Corpus with Metadata

Balázs Indig[1], Árpád Knap[2], Zsófia Sárközi-Lindner[1], Mária Timári[1], Gábor Palkó[1]
[1]Eötvös Loránd University, Centre of Digital Humanities
Múzeum krt. 6-8., H-1088, Budapest, Hungary
[2]Eötvös Loránd University, Faculty of Social Sciences, Research Center for Computational Social Science
Pázmány Péter stny. 1/A, H-1117, Budapest, Hungary
{indig.balazs,lindner.zsofia,zimanyi.maria,palko.gabor}@btk.elte.hu, knap.arpad@tatk.elte.hu

Abstract

In this article, we present the method we used to create a middle-sized corpus using targeted web crawling. Our corpus contains news portal articles along with their metadata, that can be useful for diverse audiences, ranging from digital humanists to NLP users. The method presented in this paper applies rule-based components that allow the curation of the text and the metadata content. The curated data can thereon serve as a reference for various tasks and measurements. We designed our workflow to encourage modification and customisation. Our concept can also be applied to other genres of portals by using the discovered patterns in the architecture of the portals. We found that for a systematic creation or extension of a similar corpus, our method provides superior accuracy and ease of use compared to *The Wayback Machine*, while requiring minimal manpower and computational resources. Reproducing the corpus is possible if changes are introduced to the text-extraction process. The standard TEI format and Schema.org encoded metadata is used for the output format, but we stress that placing the corpus in a digital repository system is recommended in order to be able to define semantic relations between the segments and to add rich annotation.

Keywords: webarchiving, corpus, metadata, trusted digital repository, semantic web, TEI XML, schema.org

Motto:

"It is hard to imagine how one might study the history of the developed world in the late twentieth and early twenty-first century without recourse to the archived web." (J. Winters)

1. Introduction

In the glossary of the handbook entitled *The Digital Humanities*, Gardiner and Musto (2015, 250) define web archiving as "the process of collecting portions of the *World Wide Web* to ensure the information is preserved in an *Archive* for future researchers, historians and the public". It is telling, however, that in the chapter focusing on digital archives as source materials of the present scholarly practices, born-digital archives and web archives are entirely omitted, as the authors solely speak about curated digital collections designed by (digital) archivists for the research community. Web archives are much less organised and curated then digital libraries or databases, and for this reason, are far less usable for (and used by) scholars. If Gardiner and Musto (2015) are right in their choice to emphasise the role of these digital sources in answering present scholarly questions, the fact that web archives do not play a significant role among these sources is a substantial problem for the digital humanities. There are several reasons why web archives are under-represented in the scholarly use of digital sources. The main reason is the lack of high-quality metadata, as source materials must have – among others – a publication date and its authors identified by the archival institution, otherwise, the reference to the material (be it paper-based or *born-digital*) is questionable[1]. The second reason is the uniqueness and authenticity of the records. Web archives usually contain many nearly identical versions of the "same" resource. This problem is exacerbated by the nearly inseparable dirt (recurring boilerplate text) among relevant content. The drawbacks arising from the unstructured nature of a web archive hinder its integration into the network of digital cultural heritage (DCH).

As suggested in (Weber, 2018), the limitations of web archives can be described along two main dimensions: accuracy and completeness. It is very difficult to tell if an archive actually captures *all* the content on the web *accurately* related to a specific topic.

Our method, by using websites' own archives, creates "complete snapshots" of their real content from time to time, which provides real populational data for the portals included in the project. This also means that the `ELTE.DH` corpus contains all documents from the selected portals' archives which were publicly available at crawling time.

Beyond creating a corpus for NLP applications, our work focuses on providing solutions to the aforementioned issues by developing a trusted digital repository complying with *Linked Open Data technology*. Our goal with this repository is to meet the essential demands of NLP, DCH and other disciplines uniformly.

2. Background

When it comes to crawling, web archiving or corpus creation, there are a number of options. The ISO/TR 14873:2013 standard describes the details of such workflows, however, distinct disciplines have come up with their own solutions ignoring this standard or only partially adhering to it. Holding on to the terminologies of the standard, we have conducted *selective web archiving* that is enriched with more and better metadata compared to *general crawling*. We argue that our method has a smaller footprint while

[1]Winters (2017, 240) deals with the problem of website dates in detail.

remaining easy to manage. This makes the whole workflow sustainable and scalable. In the following sections, we will review the already available tools and formats to place our solution among them.

2.1. Metadata

The standardisation process of web archiving practices, initiated and controlled mainly by national libraries (Oury and Poll, 2013), does not provide comprehensive guidelines to the standardised encoding of the texts extracted from web archiving activity. The situation is much better on the level of metadata. The technical report of *Statistics and Quality Indicators for Web Archiving* stresses the importance of different metadata types for curating web resources[2]: "Long term preservation also includes keeping safe the metadata associated with the resources in the Web Archive, which are critical for supporting collection management, access and preservation activities" (ISO/TC 46/SC 8 N).

The Metadata Encoding and Transmission Standard (METS) distinguishes four metadata types to be used in curated collections sourced from web archiving: (a) Descriptive metadata, (b) Structural metadata, (c) Provenance metadata, (d) Rights metadata. This is the theoretical standpoint, but since the creation of such metadata requires a lot of manual work, it is impossible to find a collection of archived web documents that complies with these requirements on metadata entirely. Therefore, there is virtually no reliable digital cultural heritage source for researchers. In contrast, there are metadata standards which cover fine-grained requirements. The only standard that could gain large-scale adoption is *Dublin Core*, which is not refined enough to comply with the aforementioned standards. Our repository uses Schema.org, a metadata standard we have chosen for several reasons:

- Schema.org is designed explicitly for storing information about web resources
- It has a dynamic, community based development (in contrast with robust standards, such as METS)
- It is increasingly popular on the web, which makes it easy to extract metadata from the HTML source
- It is compatible with semantic web technology (Linked Open Data)
- It has a growing usage in the digital cultural heritage domain (e.g. Europeana)

2.2. Existing Hungarian Corpora

The Szeged corpus is the largest, manually annotated corpus (Vincze et al., 2010) in the Hungarian language containing 1.2 million tokens, KorKorpusz (31,492 tokens) is similar but smaller corpus based on a recent pilot project (Vadász, 2020). The first Hungarian gigaword corpus was the *Hungarian Gigaword Corpus* (Oravecz et al., 2014) with 1,532,933,778 tokens. Both aforementioned corpora contain text only from curated sources (newspapers, literary texts, social media, legal texts, etc.) that are not entirely from the Internet. The first Hungarian web corpus that was created by Kornai and his colleagues (Halácsy et al., 2004) is called the *Hungarian Webcorpus*. It was later superseded by the 1.2 billion token *Pázmány corpus*[3] (Endrédy and Prószéky, 2016) and the 2.5 billion token *HuTenTen corpus* (Jakubíček et al., 2013), two larger corpora entirely from the web. Nowadays, large corpora are utilising the *Common Crawl archive* like the OSCAR corpus (Ortiz Suárez et al., 2019) with 5.16 billion (2.33 billion deduplicated) words in Hungarian. However, the documents presented in these corpora often contain gaps due to deduplication.

All of these corpora – except the ones based on Common Crawl – have the same flaw, namely that after their creation and publication, several errors were discovered in the tools used to create them, and these errors could not be corrected as expected. The reason being that their original source HTML files have been deleted – and these are unavailable in an unmodified form on the web.

Since then, there have been numerous attempts to create web-based corpora, but these were not published and could not arouse public interest, as web corpora and crawling became increasingly common tools. The speciality of the corpus and the method presented in this paper lies in the fact that it unites the experience from the above mentioned corpora into a manually curated gigaword web corpus, which includes metadata and can be built from the source of the downloaded web pages in a reproducible manner.

3. From the web to a corpus

To put our method into a larger perspective, in the following sections we will describe the process of corpus creation in an abstract workflow (see Figure 1.), where the elements have to be further specified by certain design decisions.

3.1. The Web Crawler

Classical web crawling can be characterised by only a few parameters that are set at the start of the process. These parameters include the initial seed of URLs where to start the crawl from, the maximal depth, and the breadth to restrict the crawler's movement. In some cases a set of targeted domains is also specified. Although there are only a few widely used crawler engines, it is hard to characterize these as most web libraries (e.g. `Python requests`, `wget`, etc.) can be used for crawling nowadays and the desired output varies from corpora to "exact offline duplicates" of websites. Here we would like to mention three crawler engines: both *Heritix*[4] and *Apache Nutch* (Laliwala and Shaikh, 2013) are used in the *Internet Archive* and *Common Crawl* projects. The third crawler engine is *Spiderling* (Suchomel and Pomikálek, 2012), which was developed by the authors of Sketch Engine (Kilgarriff et al., 2014). These crawlers are fast, generalised tools, but for targeted or spe-

[2] http://netpreserve.org/resources/IIPC_project-SO_TR_14873__E__2012-10-02_DRAFT.pdf

[3] The Pázmány corpus was the first Hungarian corpus which separated edited text (news articles) from unedited text (comments).

[4] https://github.com/internetarchive/heritrix3

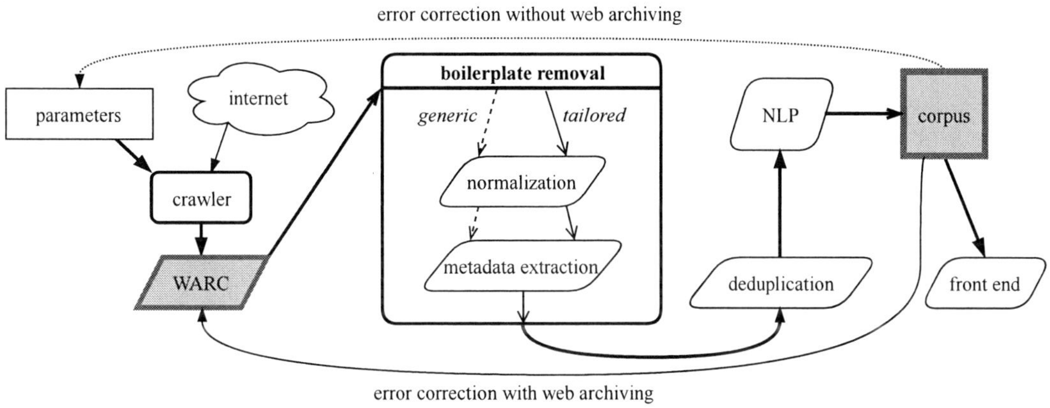

Figure 1: The abstract workflow of web corpus creation. Parallelogram-shaped boxes denote the optional phases, the grey background denotes the produced data.

cialised crawling they became tedious to use. This may explain the numerous different libraries used for crawling. Nowadays, we do not even have to use a crawler as we can begin the process with *Common Crawl*, *The Internet Archive* and similar resources. In this case, the first step is to clean the actual data, and remove collected garbage. Due to the nature of the internet, there are numerous aggressive SEO traps out in the web that are used to optimise the page rank in search engines that end up in the archive. These traps are placed in such a manner that they can divert crawler bots from their original course when these bots stumble upon them. Such general bots cannot distinguish "normal" pages from these traps, a task that humans are able to carry out in a matter of seconds. Another common problem using these sources is the need for deduplication (see Section 3.3.), which causes the waste of resources on both sides (crawler and deduplicator).

To overcome these problems, Indig et al. (2019) built a new NLP-oriented crawler tool called *Corpus Builder*, which utilises a very different approach from the above: a two-level crawling method. By using targeted crawling of large or medium portals, they claim that with their method, it is possible to crawl only the targeted portals virtually without duplication, with a small footprint and in a sustainable manner. Their main idea is the exploitation of two different levels of recurring patterns ("archives" and "article" pages) that can be discovered by analysing the structure of different web pages.

3.1.1. The Article Crawler

The first and obvious level is the recurring boilerplate content on the actual web pages of a portal. Objects of the same type are usually stored in the database back end and generated on demand into specifically formatted web pages. This is the internal nature of the data. In this paper, we call these pages "articles" regardless of their content type: whether they represent news articles, images with captions in a gallery, product descriptions and customer reviews in a webshop, posts in a forum or blog, etc. The output pages for these content types look the same in narrower time frames for a certain portal, but they can be very different from website to website. These pages are generated on the server-side, so we must collect HTMLs and extract their content. If we collect a mass amount of web pages representing the same objects from the same portal using the same template selectively or classify them after collection, the (uniform) boilerplate can be easily removed with a few simple rules per class, therefore this task does not require complex tools.

3.1.2. The Archive Crawler

The second level arises from the first: how can we systematically collect such web pages on a given portal? The answer is very simple: portals created for human readers are very likely to have some kind of a "table of contents", "product or topic list" or an "article archive", which display all available pages in a structured form. Because objects are traditionally stored in taxonomies – e.g. temporal (years, months) or other feature-based (colour, shape, price, etc.) – that can be enumerated and each object has finite number of possible values. If we enumerate articles for right feature values, we will gather links to all pages of the same layout systematically from the given portal.

3.1.3. The Possible Parameters for Portals

Using the two-step method described above, it is possible to gather a massive number of web pages even from only a small number of portals that will have virtually no duplication and effectively zero garbage pages in contrast to the general crawling methodology. This method has been successfully tested on three Hungarian news portals (Indig et al., 2019), while the further generalisation of the method for the steps following the crawling of different portals with different schemes and layouts requires further elaboration. Indig et al. (2019) assembled the minimal number of parameters that are needed to handle such portals in a unified framework. The major highlights of the configuration are showcased as the following:

- The date of the first and last article, or page number where applicable

- The archive URL format with the placeholders to be substituted
- The function for finding the *next-page URL* for the archive where applicable
- The function to get the article URLs from the archive pages
- Boolean variables to answer the following questions: is the archive paginated, infinite scrolling, or date-based?

One can distinguish between crawl-based (applicable for the current crawl), portal-based (which applies to the crawled portal regardless of crawl settings), and portal-specific configurations. Our method follows the latter direction for crawling. For problems not addressed by Indig et al. (2019) we present our solutions in Section 4.

3.2. Boilerplate Removal

There are a lot of pages that present the same type of objects or articles surrounded by the same boilerplate content (i.e. scheme or template) – menu, advertisements, etc. in a portal. In most cases, this boilerplate content can be characterised by not having multiple paragraphs with many lines of text, but containing short texts, as well as many links and pictures (Pomikálek, 2011). The process of boilerplate removal can be broken down into two steps presented in the following sections.

3.2.1. Normalisation

By normalisation we mean the reformatting of visual elements into a simpler visual annotation (e.g. the elements of Markdown language or XML tags) to create a common ground for the text of different portals in the resulting corpus. Normalisation is not a trivial task: most tools extract paragraphs as *plain text*, however, *visual formatting elements are essential* for humans and may also help the machine reader, therefore these elements should be kept and standardised.

3.2.2. Metadata extraction

Curated metadata is the cornerstone of proper (web) archiving. It can be regarded as gold standard labels for each document, which can later be utilised for training or benchmarking ML algorithms (i.e. authorship attribution, keyword extraction, topic modelling, etc.). There are automatic tools for extracting metadata from the crawled web pages such as the *Web Curator Tool*[5] or *Apache Tika*[6]. These tools extract standards compliant descriptive metadata automatically from the crawled web pages, but they are very complex and it is difficult to understand and improve their method for the specific portals. Moreover, they are plagued with the same problems as other boilerplate removal tools (see Section 3.2.3.): their heuristics and output formats are wired in by design and it is very hard to change these without major conflicts.

When the these programs yield deficient output for the targeted portals – for example due to the lack of knowledge about the typographical rules of the language, or when the output is missing some important variables, – it is inevitable to implement a custom metadata extractor methodology. We decided to use this method to allow future modifications, to be able to compare results with the presented generic tools (see Section 3.2.3.), and also to demonstrate how easily our method can be implemented. Our findings will be described in Section 4..

3.2.3. Existing Tools and Techniques

As web page layouts, coding styles, and HTML standards differ throughout the portals and were used differently over the years, the boilerplate removal task is mostly solved by clever heuristics, which makes it hard for the users to create general measurements and comparisons between them. It is also hard to set their parameters, fix, extend or modify their functionality. Some tools are designed to remove boilerplate from a single page, while others use multiple pages of the same layout to delete recurring elements (Endrédy and Novák, 2013). In this paper, we could not survey all the available methods, therefore we are comparing *JusText* (Pomikálek, 2011), a tool created directly for NLP-centric web crawling and *Newspaper3k* (Ou-Yang, 2013), created especially for news portal crawling. Both modules are still popular and widely-used because of their simplicity and effectiveness. They both remove formatting and yield plain text paragraphs, but the latter tool supports extracting metadata from web pages and has other features to simplify the crawling process for beginners.

We followed the route marked by Indig et al. (2019) and created our own handcrafted boilerplate removal rules. At first we found ourselves in a dilemma about choosing between regular expressions and HTML parsers. Regular expressions are simple, and it is also easier to train machines to create them, while HTML parsers are easier to create, read and maintain for humans, but are harder to automate. As some of the portals recently added to the corpus have very complex layouts, it is not feasible to further extend the number of portals using regular expressions. For example, it may be impossible or become very unpractical to encode various attributes and their combinations (which might be in arbitrary order due to the structure of HTML).

We compared the aforementioned methods on our gold standard data set[7]. This measurement is presented in Section 5., followed by other details of our method.

3.3. Deduplication and NLP

Sometimes the exact same content – available on several domains – can be stored in the web archive multiple times, but, of course, we need one intstance only. There are great tools for deduplication (like Onion (Pomikálek, 2011)), but their waste of valuable resources, such as disk space and network bandwidth is not ideal. When using targeted crawling, such as Indig et al. (2019), we can select only those distinct URLs which are needed and so bypass the process of deduplication.

[5] `https://webcuratortool.readthedocs.io/`

[6] `http://tika.apache.org/`

[7] Some elements were kept or thrown away by design decision that may not match with the compared tools or future use cases. However, we support the change of these decisions by the user.

The main problem with deduplication – besides wasting resources – is that some parts of a document or the whole document may become missing because it had been recognised and deleted as a duplicate. This undermines the completeness of the crawling which is the the first priority for some user groups (e.g. humanists and sociologists). The publicly available corpora that were created for NLP purposes have further disabilities: their sentences are scrambled to avoid the infringement of copyright laws. This makes the analysis of full documents – an emergent trend – impossible. The role – and legal privilege – of national libraries is to preserve documents in its entirety, even for born-digital materials. This role can be fulfilled with our method, in contrast to the traditional ones.
Different levels of NLP annotation can optionally be applied before or between the deduplication with the plethora of available tools. Until recently, texts have been stored only after this step in some format, however, the increasing performance of NLP tools makes it advisable to store crawled content also in raw format (e.g. WARC files) to be able to correct errors found in the processing pipeline. This is mainly important to humanists, sociologists and other scholars outside NLP where the specific text is the subject of analysis, in contrast to NLP, where only the amount of text matters.

3.4. The Final Format and Front End

The process of creating the output from the HTML files can be split into four steps for easier maintainability:

- *Simplification of HTML* by finding the tightest bounding HTML tag of the whole text content and decomposing unneeded subtrees[8]
- *Extraction of paragraphs and metadata* from the HTML tree keeping only specific – intended – formatting
- *Rewriting elements to a unified format* by standardising site-specific formatting
- *Writing the output file according to the expected format.* In this step, the fields get their final place and canonical names

The first three steps contain well-defined portal specific instructions, while the fourth is only dependent on the output format, which – as it is totally separated from the others – can comply with the actual purpose and front end in the future. Some user groups have special requirements, such as full documents and metadata, while others only require the raw text. Nonetheless, both requirements can be achieved at the same time.
In the field of NLP, three main use cases exist. To search patterns in large corpora, the classic vertical format used primarily by the Sketch Engine (Kilgarriff et al., 2014) is recommended. If the aim is to process the corpus with a wide variety of standard NLP tools, the CoNLL-U format[9] is adequate. If the goal is to put documents to a full text search engine or into a language model, it is necessary to comply with the input expectation of such software, which is usually raw text.
In the field of digital humanities, – especially in philology,– the XML document markup language and the Text Encoding Initiative (TEI) recommendation have become dominant over the decades (Schreibman et al., 2008). TEI makes the versioning and annotation of the enriched articles possible in an easy and reliable way, and it is also capable of storing metadata and the body of the document structurally in one file. This format satisfies NLP users as well, while opening the resulting corpus for other audiences including librarians, humanists and sociologists. TEI also allows the verification of the authenticity of the source text by the metadata and increases the reproducibility of research which has an increasing importance in the 'distant reading' paradigm (Da, 2019). Text can be converted to a simpler form corresponding to the actual use case, while keeping the master copy untouched, in a similarly to how it is done with images by resizing and cropping them on demand dynamically.

4. Method

We examined several Hungarian news portals and increased the number of examined portals to six, compared to the three portals examined by Indig et al. (2019) in order to test how the presented method can be applied to portals of different structures. First, we selected mainstream Hungarian news portals, because these contain a vast number of articles. As a secondary priority, we included portals that are special from the perspective of used web technology and architecture. We wanted to reach a milestone, where adding new portals and maintaining the existing ones is a routine task that can be handled by as little manpower as possible. In this section, we describe the main highlights of our crawling method compared to (Indig et al., 2019) (for further comparisons see Section 3.)

4.1. HTML Parsers vs. Regular Expressions

We decided to change the regular expressions used in *Corpusbuilder* (Indig et al., 2019) for Python functions, which use an HTML parser to handle the input as an HTML tree. Using HTML trees enabled us both to simplify many regular expression patterns and to support many different layouts. With this change, the accuracy of extracting article URLs from the page archives has dramatically increased, as we found that on some portals different columns may be hosted on different domains, or – while using the same site template – they may not match the expressions written for extracting URLs. This can be recognised by tree searching expressions more easily than with regular expressions. This, of course, sacrifices speed for clarity and precision, but saves us from HTML fragments slipping through regular expressions.

[8] There are three classes of decomposing rules: a) general rules used for every portal, b) "must-have" portal-specific rules, c) rules which follow certain design decisions about the data to be extracted.

[9] `https://universaldependencies.org/format.html`

4.2. The Refined Archive Crawler

The *date-based pagination handling logic* (Indig et al., 2019) was separated from other pagination methods, as it allows sorting and can be used to filter crawling by specific date intervals, since we found that date-based pagination can be and is combined freely with the other methods. We also introduced support for open (date) intervals.

Our other significant change was in handling *infinite scrolling*[10] and *active archives*[11] together in an easy-to-understand form by extracting the page URLs before determining the URL of the next archive page. We have broken down the possible patterns of finding the next archive page URL to the following cases:

- There is no pagination at all
- There is a *next page link* which we need to use
- There is *infinite scrolling*: we use the page number from the base value to "infinity" where no more article URLs are detected
- There is page numbering: we use the page number from the base value to a portal-specific maximum
- There is page numbering, but we expect the archive to expand during crawling (can be identified by finding known article URLs during crawling)

By using these features, all examined portals could be handled, therefore we narrowed down our experiments to six portals that showcase all of the described features, and allows them to be thoroughly tested.

4.3. Advanced Metadata Extraction

Metadata can be extracted from multiple sources from an article page. We identified and handled the following:

- Date, title and column are frequently encoded *in the URLs*
- HTML meta tag properties which can be encoded according to various conventions (like Dublin Core, Schema.org, etc.) that are mainly included for Search Engine Optimization (SEO) purposes
- The increasingly popular JSON-LD, storing properties that were previously stored as meta tags, but in a more structured form
- From the content of the HTML itself, where it is included to be displayed for the user

There are several portals that use more than one of the above sources of metadata. We also found examples where different sources yielded contradicting results or missing values, these are probably due to bugs in the websites' engines. Older articles tend to have more of these errors as they were probably converted from a previous layout and the conversion introduced such errors[12]. Some portals partially or fully generate metadata dynamically by using JavaScript and non-standard data-sources. This practically makes it impossible to extract such metadata with traditional tools and forces us to use a portal-specific solution.

[10] A technique used to dynamically add new content to the page when the user scrolls down.

[11] If new elements are added to the archive during crawling, the list of articles will be divided to pages in a way that their content URLs will appear on different pages than as expected. This makes it impossible to handle archive pages' URLs as permalinks.

4.4. Converting HTML to the Output Format

To handle millions of pages without reading them – through "distant reading" –, we invented utilities to examine, analyse and normalise the tags and the scheme used by a portal, and then freely convert it to the new and customisable output format. We started with cutting the HTML to the relevant part, as mentioned in Section 3.4..

The first utility function helps to *filter* out tags that do not contain any text. Next, we introduced placeholders to *simplify* some elements (e.g. links). The second function aids in *simplifying* the tags by manually selecting groups that belong to the same class (e.g. formatting, embedded content, etc.), but are specialised to the portal's scheme.

This method is quite effective even without portal-specific parameters. Table 1 shows how the number of tags (from one of the examined domains) is reduced after using these tools allowing further fine-grained modifications in an iterative manner.

	No. of tags	%
all tags	33,466	100
text containing tags	18,517	55
after simplify tags	359	10
relevant tags	267	7

Table 1: Illustration of how the number of tags to be analysed manually decreases in magnitude.

4.4.1. The Tree Representation

Possible layouts for all URLs of a domain were described with the help of a *tree-representation*: the subtrees of the contents' tightest bounding HTML tag for all pages were merged, counting the frequencies of each element and the cumulative length of their immediate text. It was also marked if a specific tag had no child elements in the tree. The resulting frequency distribution allows efficient examination and handling of subtrees for all URLs at once.

In order to be able to make decisions concerning the remaining tags, we built a *tag dictionary*. To each tag (or simplified tag), we assigned the average length of the contained text, the average number of descendants, and the average length of the immediate text supplemented with a sample of occurrences (URLs). This dictionary was augmented with the operation to perform at each occurrence of that specific tag. As we formalised the operators, their execution was made by the code automatically generated from the dictionary. These steps can be iterated to gain more insight on the portal's scheme and finally arrive to the desired form.

[12] This can be solved by crawling articles as soon as possible after their publication.

4.4.2. Rewriting Rules and Transformation Methods

When standardising and rewriting elements, we found the following operators useful:

- decomposing (deleting the tag with its contents, e.g. advertisements, boilerplate)
- unwrapping (deleting the tag, keeping its contents, e.g. text anchors)
- unwrapping all descendants (simplifying a block)
- rewriting tags context-free
- splitting tags to super-subordinate pairs (e.g. when the content and formatting properties are in the same tag)
- rewriting tags context-specific (special blocks)

These operators can be applied sequentially in the proper order for every URL. We narrowed down the various layouts (e.g. left, right, top block) into a few, portal independent types of blocks that we intended to keep. The *context-specific rules* mark the root tag for each block we found, so their subtrees can be handled by independent dictionaries in the same way. The analysis of the visual layout of the examined portals shows that there are no blocks embedded into other blocks. This property allows us to rely on the described two-level transformation with a low number of distinct tag dictionaries modified by the defined operators.

To conclude, normalising the tags and then rewriting them to the final schema are independent steps which can be achieved with successive approximation in an iterative manner. This allows us fine-grained control to change design decisions or customise the output (TEI XML in our case) easily at all times.

5. Evaluation

We ran our crawling on a low-end desktop machine (Intel i3, 4 GB RAM) for 30 days on a 100 MB/s connection (with rate-limiting to avoid the hammering of the remote servers) using circa 100 GB of disk space to demonstrate the effectivity of the method presentes here. It is not possible to compare this method's crawling performance to other general crawler engines mentioned earlier, as the workflow and methodology differ significantly (see Section 3.1.). It is possible, however, to compare the crawling accuracy to the most widely used archiving practice: the Internet Archive (see Section 5.2.). It is also possible to compare our site-specific rule-based boilerplate removal and metadata extractor functions to the mainstream crawling methods (see Section 3.2.3.).

The goal of the compared tools and their design differs significantly so the way how to make an objective comparison was not at all obvious. When comparing our method with the aforementioned tools, we strived to highlight performance differences due to design, while separating them from the strengths and weaknesses stemming from the methods themselves.

5.1. The data set

We extracted a total of 2,227,180 articles from six Hungarian news portals, this signifies 984 million words (without tokenisation) of extracted text without metadata from November 1998 until September 2019. We visualised the annual distribution of articles to see the estimated growth in the number of articles and the expected number of articles per year (see Figure 2). The figure shows a clearly growing tendency in the number of articles published on the crawled portals during the last twenty years – except 2019, which does not qualify as a full year at the time of measurement. In the case of the six portals, this means that more than 200 articles have been published on average every day in the recent years. These numbers tells us that by adding new portals the quantity of the crawled articles and the volume of the corpus can be increased quickly and easily with low human resource investment and a lightweight technical infrastructure.

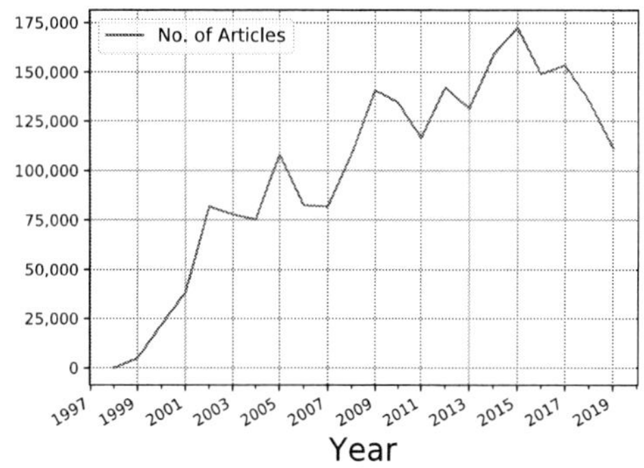

Figure 2: The annual distribution of 2,227,180 articles from six portals from November 1998 to September 2019. The number of articles per year is increasing. The decrease at 2019 is due to the fact that it is not a full year at the time of measurement.

In Table 2, we can see the performance of the boilerplate removal tools in different scenarios. We examined *JusText* and *Newspaper3k* on the full HTML code, the article body and constrained to the original and the cleaned up paragraphs. We wanted to check whether an educated initial guess (on the text's location) helps these programs or not. As the former package does not extract metadata separately, we present numbers with metadata and provide the number of words without metadata in brackets. The numbers have some small differences that suggests that a more detailed evaluation of the content is needed. We also compared the actual values of the extracted metadata (author, publication date, title) in terms of precision and recall for *Newspaper3k* (see Table 3). Our educated initial guess does not help metadata extraction, but for the text extraction it has a potential because it rules out unwanted content in one step. It is clear from these that our method is superior to the compared ones, however, a content-based comparison of the extracted paragraphs is needed in order to be able to evaluate the mentioned methods objectively. We argue that if full articles are chosen, the precision provided by our method is needed to ensure that the right amount and quality of texts can be extracted with the compared methods.

	Full HTML	Article Body	Paragraphs orig.	Paragraphs clean
All Text	12,99	1,757	1,085	982
Justext	1,157	1,020	919	918
Newspaper3k	992 (963)	974 (970)	919	917
Our Method				1,028 (984)

Table 2: The extracted text from different parts of the HTML with different tools in million words. *Newspaper3k* and our method is displayed with and without metadata.

	Full HTML	Article Body
Newspaper3k (precision)	0.77	0.69
Newspaper3k (recall)	0.52	0.26

Table 3: The content-wise comparison of metadata (author, title, publication date) extracted by *Newspaper3k* and our method (=1.0).

5.2. Crawling Compared to Archive.org

We compared our results of the six crawled news portals to the *Internet Archive* as the "standard" source of web archiving. We evaluated whether the same set of URLs could be acquired using the *Internet Archive*, and also compared the number of crawled articles by portals with data downloaded from *The Wayback Machine*.

In the following step, based on the mime type attribute, we removed all URLs from the *Internet Archive* data sets that represent content other than articles (e.g. images, scripts, etc.). Using the status code variable, we omitted all URLs that were not successfully downloaded for some reason (e.g. 404 errors and redirections). From our crawl we selected the timestamp of the last article downloaded for each domain, and removed all URLs from the *Internet Archive* data that were crawled after that date.

At this point, we still had hundreds of thousands of URLs in the *Internet Archive* data sets that represented e.g. certain taxonomy pages (date, category, author, search, etc.) or any kind of content other than single articles. Thus, we introduced a domain-level cleaning function for each crawled website, in order to remove all URLs representing content other than articles. This proved to be a difficult, time-consuming, iterative task, as in case of some websites, the URL structure changed multiple times over the years, making it nearly impossible to retrospectively identify URLs that certainly lead to articles. This is one important aspect why our method is much easier to use (even retrospectively), when the goal is to produce a clean corpus, without duplicated content. In the case of several websites, the URL structure was not logically constructed (e.g. tag archives have the same URL structure as articles; randomly generated version numbers appear at the end of some of the URLs, but not all of them; etc.), therefore in some cases, we had to restrict the comparison to certain columns of the portal, as it was very difficult to clean the data sets in a more generalised way.

Our next step was to normalise all URLs in both crawls. We removed http, https, www from the beginning, and port numbers (e.g. ":80") and parameters from the end of the URL strings. Using these normalised URLs, we created two dictionaries to store the URLs themselves and their slugs – the last part of the URL (after the last /) – for each portal. For some portals the URLs could not be used for a valid comparison, because the URL structure has changed over time, but not the slug, therefore – in these cases – we used the slug for our comparison.

With the steps described above, we reduced the number of *Archive.org* URLs from 8.9 million to only 1.2 million for the six crawled portals. After removing entries with wrong status codes 75.4%, after mime-type-based cleaning 53.7% of the URLs remained. While only 0.7% of URLs were removed in the date-based cleaning phase, after running website-specific cleaning functions and compiling the final list of URLs, just 13.5% of the initial number of URLs remained. We found that 846,343 articles are present both in our crawl and in the *Internet Archive's* data, while 1,082,484 articles are only present in the `ELTE.DH` corpus. A further 315,649 articles are only found in *Archive.org's* data. More work is needed in order to eliminate all possible bad URLs, however, it is safe to say that by using our crawler it is easier to achieve the same results than finding and downloading all relevant content from *Archive.org*.

6. Conclusion and Future Work

We have demonstrated that by using a low-end machine – which has similar computational power as our smartphones, the storage capacity of our pendrives nowadays – and minimal manpower it is possible to create a gold-standard quality gigaword corpus with metadata which suits many audiences at the same time[13]. As the presented work was only a pilot study to design and stabilise the workflow on many candidate pages, we plan to apply this methodology on several more websites, and start serving requests on site-specific crawling to provide data for research in multiple disciplines in a future version of this corpus.

In conjunction with the previously outlined plans, we intend to support national libraries with our research as they are responsible of keeping the data of our present for the future researchers who can thus provide objective and balanced research. One obvious step in this direction is to conduct research on how to keep the authenticity of web archives and how to eliminate the risks of tampering, retroactive modification and deletion of content which undermine scholarly credibility. We plan to utilise digital fingerprinting, signatures and blockchain technology on downloaded documents in order to keep them safe, while making them available for the widest possible audience.

[13]The software is published under the *GNU Lesser General Public License v3.0* at `https://github.com/ELTE-DH/WebArticleCurator` and `https://doi.org/10.5281/zenodo.3755323`

7. Bibliographical References

Da, N. Z. (2019). The computational case against computational literary studies. *Critical inquiry*, 45(3):601–639.

Endrédy, I. and Novák, A. (2013). More effective boilerplate removal-the goldminer algorithm. *Polibits*, 1(48):79–83.

Gardiner, E. and Musto, R. G. (2015). *The Digital Humanities: A Primer for Students and Scholars*. Cambridge University Press.

Indig, B., Kákonyi, T., and Novák, A. (2019). Crawling in reverse – lightweight targeted crawling of news portals. In Marek Kubis, editor, *Proceedings of the 9th Language & Technology Conference: Human Language Technologies as a Challenge for Computer Science and Linguistics*, pages 81–87, Poznań, Poland, may. Wydawnictwo Nauka i Innowacje.

Ortiz Suárez, P. J., Sagot, B., and Romary, L. (2019). Asynchronous Pipeline for Processing Huge Corpora on Medium to Low Resource Infrastructures. In Piotr Bański, et al., editors, *7th Workshop on the Challenges in the Management of Large Corpora (CMLC-7)*, Cardiff, United Kingdom, July. Leibniz-Institut für Deutsche Sprache.

Ou-Yang, L. (2013). Newspaper3k: Article scraping and curation. `https://github.com/codelucas/newspaper`.

Oury, C. and Poll, R. (2013). Counting the uncountable: statistics for web archives. *Performance Measurement and Metrics*, 14(2):132–141.

Pomikálek, J. (2011). *Removing boilerplate and duplicate content from web corpora*. Ph.D. thesis, Masaryk university, Faculty of informatics, Brno, Czech Republic.

Schreibman, S., Siemens, R., and Unsworth, J. (2008). *A companion to digital humanities*. John Wiley & Sons.

Weber, M. S. (2018). Methods and approaches to using web archives in computational communication research. *Communication Methods and Measures*, 12(2-3):200–215.

Winters, J., (2017). *Coda: Web archives for humanities research – some reflections*, pages 238–248. UCL Press.

8. Language Resource References

Endrédy, I. and Prószéky, G. (2016). A pázmány korpusz. *Nyelvtudományi Közlemények*, 112:191–205.

Halácsy, P., Kornai, A., Németh, L., Rung, A., Szakadát, I., and Trón, V. (2004). Creating open language resources for Hungarian. In *Proceedings of the Fourth International Conference on Language Resources and Evaluation (LREC'04)*, Lisbon, Portugal, May. European Language Resources Association (ELRA).

Jakubíček, M., Kilgarriff, A., Kovář, V., Rychlý, P., and Suchomel, V. (2013). The tenten corpus family. In *7th International Corpus Linguistics Conference CL*, pages 125–127.

Kilgarriff, A., Baisa, V., Bušta, J., Jakubíček, M., Kovář, V., Michelfeit, J., Rychlý, P., and Suchomel, V. (2014). The sketch engine: ten years on. *Lexicography*, pages 7–36.

Laliwala, Z. and Shaikh, A. (2013). *Web Crawling and Data Mining with Apache Nutch*. Packt Publishing.

Oravecz, C., Váradi, T., and Sass, B. (2014). The Hungarian Gigaword corpus. In *Proceedings of the Ninth International Conference on Language Resources and Evaluation (LREC'14)*, pages 1719–1723, Reykjavik, Iceland, May. European Language Resources Association (ELRA).

Suchomel, V. and Pomikálek, J. (2012). Efficient web crawling for large text corpora. In Adam Kilgarriff et al., editors, *Proceedings of the seventh Web as Corpus Workshop (WAC7)*, pages 39–43, Lyon.

Vadász, N. (2020). KorKorpusz: kézzel annotált, többrétegű pilotkorpusz építése. In Gábor Berend, et al., editors, *XVI. Magyar Számítógépes Nyelvészeti Konferencia (MSZNY 2020)*, pages 141–154, Szeged. Szegedi Tudományegyetem, TTIK, Informatikai Intézet.

Vincze, V., Szauter, D., Almási, A., Móra, Gy., Alexin, Z., and Csirik, J. (2010). Hungarian Dependency Treebank. In *Proceedings of LREC 2010*, Valletta, Malta, May. ELRA.

Proceedings of the 12th Web as Corpus Workshop, pages 42–49
Language Resources and Evaluation Conference (LREC 2020), Marseille, 11–16 May 2020

Hypernym-LIBre: A free Web-based Corpus for Hypernym Detection

Shaurya Rawat, Mariano Rico, Oscar Corcho
Ontology Engineering Group
Universidad Politécnica de Madrid, Madrid, Spain
{srawat@delicias.dia.fi., mariano.rico@, ocorcho@fi.} upm.es

Abstract

We describe a web-based corpus for hypernym detection which consists of 32 GB of high quality English paragraphs along with their part-of-speech tagged and dependency parsed versions. One of the main advantages of this corpus is that it is available under an open license while providing similar results for training and testing on state-of-the-art methods and techniques for detecting hypernyms, which makes it a good alternative to currently used corpora which are not available freely. The corpus has been created by cleaning and pre-processing the existing UMBC web-corpus and English Wikipedia.We detail existing methods for hypernym detection and analyze the state-of-the-art techniques using our corpus as a text source. We evaluate the corpus using 5 datasets and 4 models and compare them.

Keywords: hypernym detection, NLP, web-based corpus, Hearst patterns

1. Introduction

Hyponyms are terms whose semantic field lies within that of another term, which is called its Hypernym. They capture the 'is-a' or 'type-of' relationship between terms. It is also sometimes referred to as the *umbrella term* or the *blanket term*. For example: "Spain is a country". In this case, 'Spain' is an instance of the type 'country' and therefore 'country' is its hypernym. The relationship can also exist between classes. For example: "car is a vehicle". Here, both 'car' and 'vehicle' are classes as there can be multiple types of both and this is an example of class-class relationship in hypernymy. Terms that have the same hypernym are called co-hyponyms. For example: Spain and France are co-hyponyms as they have the same hypernym, country.

The earliest attempts at detecting hypernym pairs from text started with the introduction of Hearst patterns (Hearst, 1992). This approach attempted to extract the hypernyms from the text using lexico-synctactic patterns that could capture the contexts in which hyponym-hypernym pairs occur in text. These patterns take advantage of noun phrases in a given corpus. Even though Hearst patterns may capture the hyponym-hypernym pairs from the corpus, they suffer from sparsity, that is, if the pairs do not follow the exact pattern that is used, then no relation is picked up.

Recent works are now moving to the distributional methods for hypernym detection which are based on the **DIH (distributional inclusion hypotheses)** (Geffet and Dagan, 2005), which states that the contexts in which a narrower term like 'Spain' occurs should be a subset of the contexts in which the broader term 'country' occurs. The measures in this space follow on from the creation of distributional semantic spaces and then use inclusion (Weeds et al., 2004) or non-inclusion (Lenci and Benotto, 2012) measures to detect if the hypernym relation holds. There is an alternative to the inclusion hypotheses, called the **informativeness** hypotheses, which uses entropy instead of inclusion contexts. This has been covered in Santus et al. (2014) and furthered in Shwartz et al. (2016b). Along with distributional approaches, there are some machine learning based approaches that introduce the idea of using dependency paths as features for known hypernym pairs (Snow et al., 2005) and further work branching out from this using satellite links (Sheena et al., 2016). Both referenced works train a classifier to predict whether the relation holds between two terms. There has also been work in the field of using distributional semantic spaces called embeddings (Mikolov et al., 2013; Pennington et al., 2014) to train classifiers for predicting hypernymy.

Recent works on hypernym detection have used Wikipedia derived corpora (Shwartz et al., 2016a) or Gigaword (Graff, David, and Christopher Cieri, 2011) concatenated with Wikipedia (Roller et al., 2018). Evaluation of extractions from these corpora has been done using 5 datasets which will be covered later in this paper (Section 3.2.3). Being consistent with Roller et al. (2018) and Shwartz et al. (2016b), average precision is used as a metric to evaluate extractions and predict hypernymy between pairs in all datasets.

In this paper, we first describe the two corpora from which our corpus is derived. We also detail the various approaches to hypernym detection and our methodology in extracting candidate pairs from the corpus. Finally, we describe the evaluation datasets used and compare our results to the current state-of-the-art (Roller et al., 2018).

We propose a free corpus along with its POS-tagged and dependency parsed versions that produces similar results on 5 tests and 4 methods. This is the main contribution of the paper [1] along with the relevant code for implementation [2], and the hyponym-hypernym pairs extracted.

2. Corpus Description

Our corpus has been created as a concatenation of two web-based sources that are provided not only in their raw format but also POS-tagged with dependency path annotations using spacy (Honnibal and Montani, 2017). Both sources are described in the following sections.

[1]DOI: 10.5281/zenodo.3662204

[2]https://github.com/abyssnlp/Hypernym-LIBre

2.1. UMBC Web Corpus

The UMBC [3] corpus (Han et al., 2013) is based on the Stanford WebBase crawl from February 2007 and contains 100 million web pages from 50,000 websites. Duplicated paragraphs and non-English words as well as strange characters were removed from the text to get 3 billion good quality English words. The corpus can be downloaded freely as a 13GB tar file which when uncompressed, comes to around 48GB of text + part-of-speech tagged files. There are 408 files which contain English text in the paragraph format and 408 files that are the same paragraphs but part-of-speech tagged.

2.2. Wikipedia Corpus

The English Wikipedia corpus is a widely used corpus in the field of Computational Linguistics and Natural Language Processing. It provides data for various fields of research as a one-stop online free encyclopedia. It also provides various APIs for extracting specific information and the entire Wikipedia in downloadable format [4] either in XML or SQL for directly integrating into a database for further analyses. Wikipedia as a corpus is especially useful in the field of Hypernym detection because it covers a variety of topics which can be extracted as candidate pairs for satisfying the relation.

2.3. Part-of-Speech Tagging and Dependency Parsing of our corpus

The UMBC corpus comes with 408 files of POS-tagged version of the their text counterparts which is almost 30GB. According to Han et al. (2013), the corpus was POS-tagged using the Stanford POS Tagger (Toutanova and Manning, 2000). As the POS-tagged version of UMBC is quite dated and we needed to POS-tag Wikipedia as well to extract noun-phrases from the corpora, we used the multi-task CNN(Convolutional Neural Network) from spacy (Honnibal and Montani, 2017) for the concatenation of both. Although we do not use dependency parsing in our models or experiments, it is useful for implementing some distributional models as listed in Shwartz et al. (2016b). We therefore, provide the dependency parsed version of the corpus as well for aiding future research in this field. This has also been performed using the dependency parser available in spacy.

3. Hypernym Detection

We analyze the state-of-the-art pattern-based methods for hypernym detection from Roller et al. (2018) and our evaluation shows that the results using our corpus are similar to the results from the alternate paid corpus mentioned before.

3.1. Approaches for Hypernym Detection

There are 3 main groups of approaches for hypernym detection that we enlist below.

[3] https://ebiquity.umbc.edu/blogger/2013/05/01/umbc-webbase-corpus-of-3b-english-words/

[4] https://dumps.wikimedia.org/

3.1.1. Pattern Based Methods

Pattern-based methods are the current state-of-the-art in Hypernym detection (Roller et al., 2018).
These methods use lexico-syntactic patterns (LSPs) to extract hypernym pairs based on their linguistic structure. The most popular patterns were proposed by Hearst (1992), as shown in Table 1, where NP stands for noun phrases. Apart from the regular Hearst Patterns, more patterns can be used to extract hypernym-hyponyms from a corpus.

3.1.2. Unsupervised Distributional Methods

These methods involve the formation of distributional semantic spaces or DSMs to capture the contexts in which a word occurs. It is closely linked to how word embeddings like Word2Vec (Mikolov et al., 2013) or GloVe (Pennington et al., 2014) are formed.
A vector space is created based on these contexts, and can be used to determine whether two words hold the hypernym relation.Vector spaces can be created using window-based approaches(taking a fixed window around the target word) or dependency-tree based(taking the parent and sister node of the target word in a dependency tree). For example, Let us consider a sentence: "Trade laws in **Uganda** are similar to those in South Africa." In this sentence, if we do not know what **Uganda** is, looking at the contexts surrounding this word and projecting it into a vector space of similar contexts, we can infer that it must be a country. A common method for checking for similarity in distributional spaces is Cosine Similarity (Dillon, 1983). After the creation of such a distributional semantic space, various measures can be applied for hypernymy detection. All measures are variants of the DIH (Distributional Inclusion Hypothesis) (Geffet and Dagan, 2005), which states that a narrower term's contexts will always be a subset of the broader term's contexts. For example: The context in which a narrower term like *dog* appears will be always be a subset of the contexts of a broader term like *animal*. All DIH measures are defined for large, sparse and positively valued distributional spaces. There are 3 main variants based on this:

- *WeedsPrec* (Weeds et al., 2004) which captures contexts of x that are included in the set of a broader term's contexts like y

$$WeedsPrec(x, y) = \frac{\sum_{i=1}^{n} x_i * \mathbb{1}_{y_i} > 0}{\sum_{i=1}^{n} x_i} \quad (1)$$

- *invCL* (Lenci and Benotto, 2012) which uses distributional inclusion as well as distributional exclusion of the contexts of the two words. It uses the inclusion variant from Clarke (2009) and adds a non-inclusion element to it.

$$CL(x, y) = \frac{\sum_{i=1}^{n} min(x_i, y_i}{\sum_{i=1} nx_i} \quad (2)$$

	Hearst Patterns
Pattern #1	NP_0 *such as* $NP_1, NP_2 \ldots, (and \mid or)\ NP_n$ Example: " Countries such as Spain, France and Germany." Extracts: NP_0: Countries (hypernym), NP_1: Spain (hyponym), NP_2: France (hyponym)
Pattern #2	*such* NP_0 *as* $\{NP_1,\} * \{(or \mid and)\}\ NP_n$ Example: "such flowers as Hibiscus and Rose." Extracts: NP_0: Flowers (hypernym), NP_1: Hibiscus (hyponym) and NP_2: Rose (hyponym)
Pattern #3	$NP_0\ \{, NP_1\} * \{,\}$ *or other* NP_2 Example: "Enid Blyton, Mario Puzo or other authors." Extracts: NP_0: Enid Blyton (hyponym), NP_1: Mario Puzo (hyponym), NP_2: authors (hypernym)
Pattern #4	$NP_0\ \{, NP_1\} * \{,\}$ *and other* NP_2 Example: "Socrates, Plato and other philosophers." Extracts: NP_0: Socrates (hyponym), NP_1: Plato (hyponym), NP_2: philosophers (hypernym)
Pattern #5	$NP_0\ \{,\}$ *including* $\{NP_1,\} * \{or \mid and\} NP_2$ Example: "Fishes including Dolphins and Rays." Extracts: NP_0: Fishes (hypernym), NP_1: Dolphins (hyponym), NP_2: Rays (hyponym)
Pattern #6	$NP_0\ \{,\}$ *especially* $\{NP_1,\} * \{or \mid and\} NP_2$ Example: "East European countries especially Bosnia and Hungary." Extracts: NP_0: East_European_countries (hypernym), NP_1: Bosnia (hyponym), NP_2: Hungary (hyponym)

Table 1: Hearst Patterns, Marti Hearst(1992).

$$invCL(x,y) = \sqrt{CL(x,y) * (1 - CL(y,x)} \quad (3)$$

- *SLQS* (Santus et al., 2014; Shwartz et al., 2016b) which is based on the alternate **informativeness** hypothesis. It depends on the median entropy of a term's top N contexts. Here N becomes the hyperparameter for the model.

$$E_x = median_{i=1}^{N}[H(c_i)] \quad (4)$$

, where H is the Shannon entropy. Then SLQS model is defined as the ratio of its application on both the terms in the pair:

$$SLQS(x,y) = 1 - \frac{E_x}{E_y} \quad (5)$$

3.1.3. Machine Learning Based Approaches

Supervised learning methods have been used to classify whether two words hold the hypernymy relation or not. Methods such as in Snow et al. (2005) and Sheena et al. (2016), create a training set with dependency paths between known hypernym-hyponym pairs as the features and the target as a binary variable whether that dependency path leads to a hypernymy relation or not. This task then becomes a binary classification task and can be used as a Hypernym classifier between a pair of words, given the dependency path that links them.

There has been recent progress in using neural networks and spherical embeddings (Wang et al., 2019) and in combining pattern-based approaches with nearest-neighbor candidate pairs (Held and Habash, 2019). However, these have not been considered in this study and are beyond the scope of this paper.

3.2. A Pattern-based Methodology for Hypernym Detection

Roller et al. (2018) conclude that pattern-based methods outperform distributional methods for Hypernym detection. In order to validate extractions, a corpus is required to match the patterns and obtain candidate hypernym-hyponym pairs. The dataset used in Roller et al. (2018) consisted of the concatenation of the Gigaword (Graff, David, and Christopher Cieri, 2011) and the Wikipedia corpus.

However, Gigaword is a paid corpus and requires fees for access. We used an alternate corpus derived from the concatenation of the UMBC and the Wikipedia corpus. A relevant result is that using our free corpus, we were able to achieve similar state-of-the-art results for all the datasets the extractions were validated on.

We now outline our methodology for obtaining these results using Pattern-based methods for Hypernym detection.

3.2.1. Extracting Pairs from the Corpus

Pairs were extracted from the UMBC+Wikipedia corpus as follows:

1. Convert the Hearst Patterns shown in Table 1 into regular expressions.
2. Pre-process and clean the corpus by removing special characters like #,$, HTML tags etc.
3. Split the corpus into sentences and tokenize each sentence into words such that we get a list of sentences where each sentence is a list of words.
4. Part-of-speech tag the words in each sentence with the Perceptron Tagger[5] [6].
5. Extract noun phrases from the text. Sequential noun phrases are combined into one with a single 'NP_' header
6. Match Hearst Patterns with the text and extract hyponym-hypernym pairs.

3.2.2. Matrix Operations on the Extractions

After extracting the pairs from the corpus, we compress them to get each unique pair and the frequency of extraction from the total extractions. This creates a counts table where we have the pair extracted alongside the number of times (frequency) of occurrence.
From these pairs and counts, we create a sparse co-occurrence matrix of all the words in the vocabulary where the rows are the hyponyms from each pair and the columns are the hypernyms. The value of each cell in the matrix is the number of extractions of that particular hyponym-hypernym pair or the frequency.
The *Raw Count Matrix* is created by dividing each value in the matrix by the total number of extractions to get the raw probability of extracting that particular pair as a valid hyponym-hypernym pair.
Let ρ denote the set of extractions from corpus τ ,

$$\rho = \{(x, y)\}_{i=1}^{n} \tag{6}$$

Let $w(x, y)$ denote the count of how often (x,y) has been extracted using our patterns from the corpus and the total number of extractions W be denoted as:

$$W = \sum_{(x,y)\in\rho} w(x, y) \tag{7}$$

In order to predict the hypernymy relation using this raw count matrix, we will use the probability of extraction of the pair as:

$$p(x, y) = \frac{w(x, y)}{W} \tag{8}$$

This is detailed in Algorithm 1.
However, raw count probabilities for predicting this relation suffers from word occurrence inconsistencies. For example, $(humans, mammals)$ are more likely to be extracted from the corpus than $(human, vertebrates)$, but both are true for hypernymy as humans are both mammals and vertebrates.
To deal with this, Roller et al. (2018) also used *PPMI (Positive Pointwise Mutual Information)* which is the mathematical translation of how likely are two words to occur together than occur independent of each other. We only take positive examples in this case as hypernymy is an asymmetric relationship. Although similarity is one of its properties, for example: blue is a color but the reverse is not true. As defined in Roller et al. (2018),

$$p^{-}(x) = \frac{\sum_{(x,y)\in\rho} w(x, y)}{W} \tag{9}$$

$$p^{+}(x) = \frac{\sum_{(y,x)\in\rho} w(y, x)}{W} \tag{10}$$

where, $p^{-}(x)$ and $p+(x)$ are the probability that x occurs as a hyponym and hypernym respectively.
Then the PPMI for the extracted pair (x,y) can be computed as:

$$ppmi(x, y) = max(0, log\frac{p(x, y)}{p^{-}(x)p^{+}(y)}) \tag{11}$$

The PPMI matrix is implemented on the raw count matrix as show in Algorithm 2.
While this can deal with skewed word occurrence probabilities, we still cannot handle out-of-vocabulary or unseen pairs. Therefore, we compute low-rank embeddings of the PPMI and the raw count matrix so that we can generalize to unseen or new pairs. Towards this, we use SVD or *Singular Value decomposition*, which is a kind of matrix factorization and reduces the matrix on the basis of the hyperparameter k which captures the number of singular values to retain and truncates all the rest. This leads to similar words having similar representations.
Given,
Let SVD of matrix M,

$$M = U\sum V^{T} \tag{12}$$

Then, Truncated SVD of M,

$$Trunc.SVD = u_x^{T} \sum_{r} v_y \tag{13}$$

in which all but the r largest singular values are set to 0.
In the experiments, we consider the SVD of both the raw count as well as the PPMI matrix. Implementation and procedure are detailed in Algorithm 3.

3.2.3. Evaluation Datasets

The 5 datasets used in the evaluation of our pattern-based methods are consistent with Roller et al. (2018) and Shwartz et al. (2016b).
Below we outline and detail the 5 datasets used:

[5]https://www.nltk.org/_modules/nltk/tag/perceptron.html

[6]Please note that while running the experiment, we POS tagged the corpus using the Perceptron Tagger. As the spacy tagger has been shown to be perform better, we POS tagged Hypernym-LIBre with it before releasing it as a language resource.

Algorithm 1 Raw Count Matrix from Hearst Patterns

$p \leftarrow (x, y)_{i=1}^{n}$ ▷ (x,y) - hyponym,hypernym pairs
$w(x, y) \leftarrow freq(x, y)$ ▷ frequency of extraction
$W \leftarrow \sum_{(x,y)\in p} w(x, y)$ ▷ total extractions
for $i := 1 \rightarrow n$ **do**
    $P(x_i, y_i) \leftarrow \frac{w(x_i, y_i)}{W}$
end for

Algorithm 2 PMI (Pointwise Mutual Information) on Raw Count Matrix

$p^{-}(x) \leftarrow \sum_{row} x$ ▷ prob(x as hyponym)
$p^{+}(x) \leftarrow \sum_{col} x$ ▷ prob(x as hypernym)
$p(x, y) \leftarrow \frac{w(x,y)}{W}$ ▷ from Algorithm 1
for $i := 1 \rightarrow n$ **do**
    $PMI(x_i, y_i) \leftarrow log\frac{p(x_i, y_i)}{p^{-}(x_i)\cdot p^{+}(y_i)}$
end for

1. BLESS (Baroni and Lenci, 2011)
   This dataset contains hypernymy annotations for around 200 nouns. It contains pairs for other relations like meronymy and co-hyponymy as well. We label the hypernym pairs as true and all other relations as false. It contains 14,542 total pairs with 1,337 positive examples.

2. LEDS (Baroni et al., 2012)
   This dataset consists of 2,770 nouns and comes balanced with randomly shuffled positive as well as negative pairs.

3. EVAL (Santus et al., 2015)
   This dataset contains 7,378 pairs in a mixture of hypernym ,antonym and synonym pairs. We only mark the hypernym pairs as true and all other relations as false.

4. SHWARTZ (Shwartz et al., 2016a)
   This is the largest dataset used. We took a subset containing 52,578 pairs (Roller et al., 2018).

5. WBLESS (Weeds et al., 2014)
   A dataset of 1,668 subset of the BLESS dataset containing negative pairs from other close relations to confirm the validity of our predictions.

Average precision is used as metric to score all the models in this paper to be consistent with Roller et al. (2018) and Shwartz et al. (2016b).

3.2.4. Setup and Hardware

The pairs were extracted, processed and evaluated on a server with 8 Intel Xeon cores and 64 GB of RAM .
None of the models have a hyper-parameter except for SVD based models, for which we selected k=100 for all. We also performed experiments with various other values of k={10,20,50,100,1000} but they have been omitted from the results for the sake of brevity.

3.2.5. Results and Comparison

Our evaluation shows that the results using our corpus are similar to the results from the alternate paid corpus mentioned before. Prior to evaluating, we trim all the extractions from our corpus that are less than 2 as it helps control the sparsity of our extractions. Truncated SVD on the PPMI models achieve highest scores overall. This is due to its matrix completion properties as similar words have similar representations. There are some slight variations in the results which stem from the difference in the corpus used and/or the pre-processing methodologies. However, these slight variations are not unidirectional as we perform slightly better in some datasets and slight worse in others. Overall, the results are similar as can be seen in Table 2. The metric used here is average precision. It summarizes the precision-recall curve with the weighted mean of precision at each threshold, with the increase in recall from the previous threshold used as the weight.

$$AP(AveragePrecision) = \sum_{n}(R_n - R_{n-1})P_n \quad (14)$$

, where R_n and P_n are recall and precision at the nth threshold.
The comparison is as detailed below (the darker bars with suffix '_sota' represent the results from Roller et al. (2018) and the lighter bars with suffix '_libre' represent our results):

1. BLESS Dataset

   On the BLESS dataset, we perform similar to Roller et al. (2018). Here, SVD applied on the PPMI matrix achieves an Average Precision score of 0.71 as compared to 0.76. (as shown in Figure 1)

2. LEDS Dataset

   Similarly in LEDS, some of our models outperform Roller et al. (2018) and achieve exact scores on the highest performing SVD on PPMI matrix model. LEDS contains noun pairs which are discriminative and hence we get high scores overall. (as shown in Figure 2)

3. EVAL Dataset
   This dataset has some out-of-vocabulary words with

Algorithm 3 SVD (Singular Value Decomposition) on Raw Count and PPMI Matrix

$C \leftarrow raw\ count\ matrix/PPMI\ matrix$ ▷ from Algorithm 1/2
$k \leftarrow 100$ ▷ hyperparameter k
$r \leftarrow rank(C)$
$SVD(C) \leftarrow U \cdot \sum \cdot V^T$
$\sum_k \subset \sum$ ▷ truncated SVD by selecting k=100 singular values
$C_k \leftarrow U \cdot \sum_k \cdot V^T$ ▷ final matrix to use for predictions

Datasets	Result Comparison							
	Models							
	Raw Count Model		PPMI Model		SVD Raw Count Model		SVD PPMI Model	
	SOTA	LIBre	SOTA	LIBre	SOTA	LIBre	SOTA	LIBre
BLESS	0.49	0.47	0.45	0.42	0.66	0.64	0.76	0.71
LEDS	0.71	0.73	0.7	0.73	0.81	0.82	0.84	0.84
EVAL	0.38	0.35	0.36	0.32	0.45	0.42	0.48	0.42
SHWARTZ	0.29	0.36	0.28	0.33	0.41	0.53	0.44	0.47
WBLESS	0.74	0.74	0.72	0.73	0.91	0.93	0.96	0.95

Table 2: Result Comparison between extractions from state-of-the-art corpus and Hypernym-LIBre.

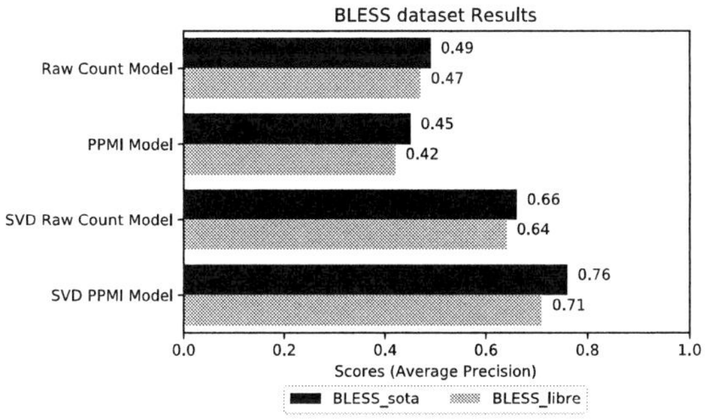

Figure 1: Pattern based methods on BLESS dataset

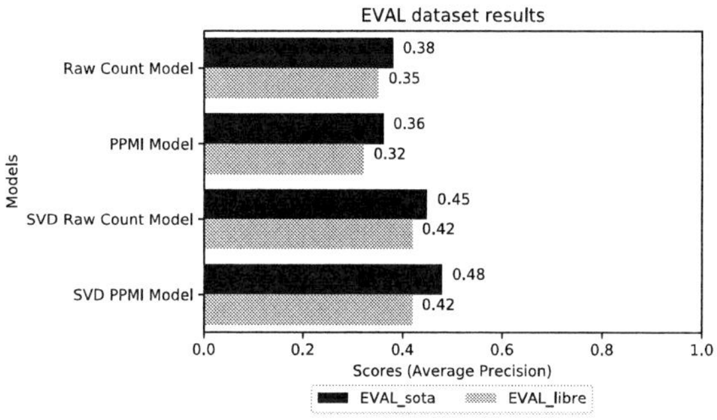

Figure 3: Pattern based methods on EVAL dataset

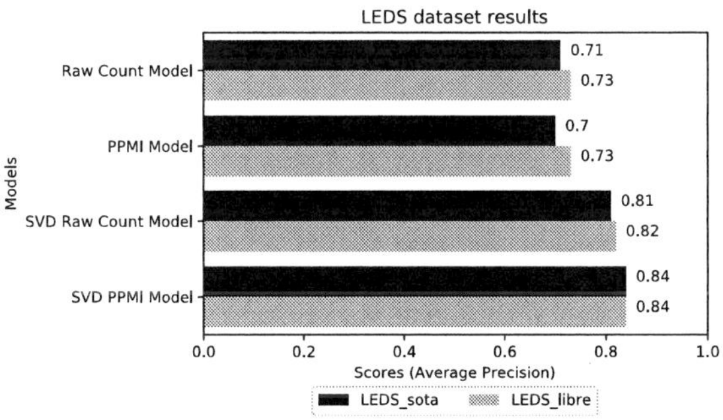

Figure 2: Pattern based methods on LEDS dataset

respect to our corpus from which we extracted our pairs and most of the pairs are verb or adjective pairs. Since our patterns extract noun pairs from the corpus, the score gets penalized by these pairs. Here we achieve 0.42 AP on the SVD PPMI model as compared to 0.48. (as shown in Figure 3)

4. SHWARTZ Dataset

This dataset is the largest dataset and it also has some

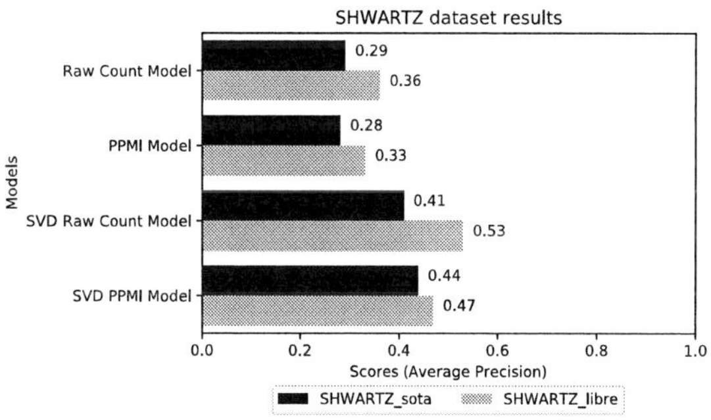

Figure 4: Pattern based methods on SHWARTZ dataset

very low frequency words which are not picked up by our Hearst Pattern based models and hence the overall score is low for all models. Here, we are at level with the state-of-the-art scores. (as shown in Figure 4)

5. WBLESS Dataset

This dataset scores very high on AP across all the

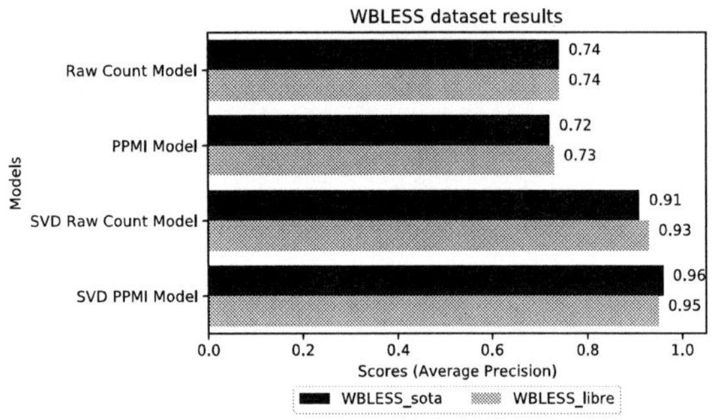

Figure 5: Pattern based methods on WBLESS dataset

models. Here, the SVD applied to PPMI matrix model achieves 0.95 AP compared to 0.96. (as shown in Figure 5)

4. Conclusion

We have created a new corpus that can be used by those working in methods and techniques for hypernym detection. Our evaluation shows that we get similar results when we apply state-of-the-art methods to it, hence showing that the corpus can be used for the same purpose as it has been done with previous corpora in the state-of-the-art, with the benefit of using a corpus that is available under an open license. In order to show that the usage of this corpus does not have a negative impact in comparison with the usage of previous ones, we also show how we applied all the pattern-based methods described in Roller et al. (2018) with our new corpus achieving similar results.
As future work, we plan to improve existing pattern-based methods using better or more patterns and generalization techniques. We also plan on testing the combination of distributional and pattern-based approaches.

5. Bibliographical References

Baroni, M. and Lenci, A. (2011). How we blessed distributional semantic evaluation. In *Proceedings of the GEMS 2011 Workshop on GEometrical Models of Natural Language Semantics*, pages 1–10. Association for Computational Linguistics.

Baroni, M., Bernardi, R., Do, N.-Q., and Shan, C.-c. (2012). Entailment above the word level in distributional semantics. In *Proceedings of the 13th Conference of the European Chapter of the Association for Computational Linguistics*, pages 23–32. Association for Computational Linguistics.

Clarke, D. (2009). Context-theoretic semantics for natural language: an overview. In *Proceedings of the workshop on geometrical models of natural language semantics*, pages 112–119.

Dillon, M. (1983). Introduction to modern information retrieval: G. salton and m. mcgill. mcgraw-hill, new york (1983). xv+ 448 pp., 32.95 isbn 0-07-054484-0.

Geffet, M. and Dagan, I. (2005). The distributional inclusion hypotheses and lexical entailment. In *Proceedings of the 43rd Annual Meeting on Association for Computational Linguistics*, pages 107–114. Association for Computational Linguistics.

Han, L., Kashyap, A. L., Finin, T., Mayfield, J., and Weese, J. (2013). Umbc_ebiquity-core: Semantic textual similarity systems. In *Second Joint Conference on Lexical and Computational Semantics (* SEM), Volume 1: Proceedings of the Main Conference and the Shared Task: Semantic Textual Similarity*, pages 44–52.

Hearst, M. A. (1992). Automatic acquisition of hyponyms from large text corpora. In *Proceedings of the 14th conference on Computational linguistics-Volume 2*, pages 539–545. Association for Computational Linguistics.

Held, W. and Habash, N. (2019). The effectiveness of simple hybrid systems for hypernym discovery. In *Proceedings of the 57th Annual Meeting of the Association for Computational Linguistics*, pages 3362–3367.

Honnibal, M. and Montani, I. (2017). spacy 2: Natural language understanding with bloom embeddings, convolutional neural networks and incremental parsing. *To appear*, 7(1).

Lenci, A. and Benotto, G. (2012). Identifying hypernyms in distributional semantic spaces. In ** SEM 2012: The First Joint Conference on Lexical and Computational Semantics–Volume 1: Proceedings of the main conference and the shared task, and Volume 2: Proceedings of the Sixth International Workshop on Semantic Evaluation (SemEval 2012)*, pages 75–79.

Mikolov, T., Sutskever, I., Chen, K., Corrado, G. S., and Dean, J. (2013). Distributed representations of words and phrases and their compositionality. In *Advances in neural information processing systems*, pages 3111–3119.

Pennington, J., Socher, R., and Manning, C. D. (2014). Glove: Global vectors for word representation. In *Proceedings of the 2014 conference on empirical methods in natural language processing (EMNLP)*, pages 1532–1543.

Roller, S., Kiela, D., and Nickel, M. (2018). Hearst patterns revisited: Automatic hypernym detection from large text corpora. *arXiv preprint arXiv:1806.03191*.

Santus, E., Lenci, A., Lu, Q., and Im Walde, S. S. (2014). Chasing hypernyms in vector spaces with entropy. In *Proceedings of the 14th Conference of the European Chapter of the Association for Computational Linguistics, volume 2: Short Papers*, pages 38–42.

Santus, E., Yung, F., Lenci, A., and Huang, C.-R. (2015). Evalution 1.0: an evolving semantic dataset for training and evaluation of distributional semantic models. In *Proceedings of the 4th Workshop on Linked Data in Linguistics: Resources and Applications*, pages 64–69.

Sheena, N., Jasmine, S. M., and Joseph, S. (2016). Automatic extraction of hypernym & meronym relations in english sentences using dependency parser. *Procedia Computer Science*, 93:539–546.

Shwartz, V., Goldberg, Y., and Dagan, I. (2016a). Improving hypernymy detection with an integrated path-based and distributional method. *arXiv preprint arXiv:1603.06076*.

Shwartz, V., Santus, E., and Schlechtweg, D. (2016b). Hypernyms under siege: Linguistically-motivated artillery for hypernymy detection. *arXiv preprint arXiv:1612.04460*.

Snow, R., Jurafsky, D., and Ng, A. Y. (2005). Learning syntactic patterns for automatic hypernym discovery. In *Advances in neural information processing systems*, pages 1297–1304.

Toutanova, K. and Manning, C. D. (2000). Enriching the knowledge sources used in a maximum entropy part-of-speech tagger. In *Proceedings of the 2000 Joint SIGDAT conference on Empirical methods in natural language processing and very large corpora: held in conjunction with the 38th Annual Meeting of the Association for Computational Linguistics-Volume 13*, pages 63–70. Association for Computational Linguistics.

Wang, C., He, X., and Zhou, A. (2019). Spherere: Distinguishing lexical relations with hyperspherical relation embeddings. In *Proceedings of the 57th Annual Meeting of the Association for Computational Linguistics*, pages 1727–1737.

Weeds, J., Weir, D., and McCarthy, D. (2004). Characterising measures of lexical distributional similarity. In *Proceedings of the 20th international conference on Computational Linguistics*, page 1015. Association for Computational Linguistics.

Weeds, J., Clarke, D., Reffin, J., Weir, D., and Keller, B. (2014). Learning to distinguish hypernyms and co-hyponyms. In *Proceedings of COLING 2014, the 25th International Conference on Computational Linguistics: Technical Papers*, pages 2249–2259. Dublin City University and Association for Computational Linguistics.

6. Language Resource References

Graff, David, and Christopher Cieri. (2011). *English Gigaword*. Linguistic Data Consortium, 5.0, ISLRN 953-543-425-922-6.

Proceedings of the 12th Web as Corpus Workshop, pages 50–56
Language Resources and Evaluation Conference (LREC 2020), Marseille, 11–16 May 2020

A Cross-Genre Ensemble Approach to Robust Reddit Part of Speech Tagging

Shabnam Behzad, Amir Zeldes
Corpling Lab
Georgetown University
shabnam@cs.georgetown.edu, amir.zeldes@georgetown.edu

Abstract

Part of speech tagging is a fundamental NLP task often regarded as solved for high-resource languages such as English. Current state-of-the-art models have achieved high accuracy, especially on the news domain. However, when these models are applied to other corpora with different genres, and especially user-generated data from the Web, we see substantial drops in performance. In this work, we study how a state-of-the-art tagging model trained on different genres performs on Web content from unfiltered Reddit forum discussions. More specifically, we use data from multiple sources: OntoNotes, a large benchmark corpus with 'well-edited' text, the English Web Treebank with 5 Web genres, and GUM, with 7 further genres other than Reddit. We report the results when training on different splits of the data, tested on Reddit. Our results show that even small amounts of in-domain data can outperform the contribution of data an order of magnitude larger coming from other Web domains. To make progress on out-of-domain tagging, we also evaluate an ensemble approach using multiple single-genre taggers as input features to a meta-classifier. We present state of the art performance on tagging Reddit data, as well as error analysis of the results of these models, and offer a typology of the most common error types among them, broken down by training corpus.

Keywords: POS, tagger, genre, domain adaptation, ensemble

1. Introduction

With the rapid growth of social media platforms and general public participation on the Internet, user-generated content has become one of the main data resources for different applications (Sanguinetti et al., 2020). Textual data from these platforms are being used in many NLP tasks even though they are often not well-structured, and deviate from prescriptive language norms. The combination of such heterogeneous data and differences with typical kinds of training data (often newswire language) are hence challenging to work with: different types of noise are introduced into these datasets because of non-standard lexical items, spelling inconsistencies, informal abbreviations, and linguistic errors (Gui et al., 2017; Meftah and Semmar, 2018).

Part of speech tagging is a fundamental NLP task which has long been studied, and, based on standard benchmarks, now seems nearly solved: for example, recent approaches have reached an accuracy of 97.85% (Akbik et al., 2018) on the Wall Street Journal corpus, essentially approaching human levels of accuracy. However, when state-of-the-art models are evaluated on out of domain data, we observe a drop in performance (Derczynski et al., 2013); this could be the result of differences in topic, writing style and epoch between training and testing data (Manning, 2011). At the same time, high quality POS tagging is particularly pertinent for non-standard language, since exposing parts of speech in unusual text types gives access to underlying categories (e.g. proper nouns, predicates) which are difficult to recognize on a textual basis when they have unusual forms. Because the resulting POS tags are frequently used as part of downstream NLP tasks, errors caused by the tagger can propagate and affect the results of these downstream tasks as well (Foster et al., 2011). Thus, NLP tasks can benefit substantially from high accuracy, domain-robust POS tagging.

Enhancing the performance of taggers for social media data in particular has been studied before. Most of these studies, however, have focused on data from Twitter, which diverges from standard language strongly, but also represents a very narrow subdomain of user-generated content. In this work, we focus on a different platform, Reddit, which has a more heterogeneous text structure from Twitter. We compare the performance of the state-of-the-art tagging framework Flair (Akbik et al., 2018) trained on different genres and tested on Reddit data, and provide a deep analysis of the errors produced in each of the models. Our initial results suggest that even small amounts of in-domain data used in training can outperform the contribution of data an order of magnitude larger but from other domains, despite the fact that most of the data sources used in this paper come from a range of Web genres themselves. In order to achieve progress on generalization to new domains, we also evaluate an ensemble model which uses the predictions of multiple models trained on different genres as features. We observe the effectiveness of these features by an ablation study and report the results.

2. Related Work

Over the past decades there has been a growing body of work focusing on POS tagging and domain adaptation. Many approaches have been proposed to improve tagging performance using different models such as Conditional Random Fields, Hidden/Maximum Entropy Markov Models, linear classifiers and neural architectures (Mueller et al., 2013; Sun, 2014; Huang et al., 2015; Choi, 2016; Qi et al., 2018; Akbik et al., 2018).

With the growth of social media and the tremendous amount of user-generated textual data available, researchers now analyze and use these data in many different NLP tasks (Liu et al., 2018). Studies show that the performance of NLP tools including POS taggers typically degrades when the models are tested on unedited text such as tweets (Ritter et al., 2011), however, retraining the models on in-domain data can improve performance (Neunerdt et al., 2013). Giesbrecht and Evert (2009) presented an evaluation of various POS taggers in German when trained on newspaper corpora and then tested on less standardized text genres such as Web corpora and observed a drop in performance. They also analyzed how tagging different web genres could present different levels of difficulty for the trained models. More specifically, they found TV episode guide, online forum, conference information and news report data to be harder than other text genres.

Studies of tagging specifically for the heterogeneous space of Reddit text remain outstanding. Previous research has studied the problem of POS tagging on social media data primarily by targeting Twitter. Some have proposed new tagging schemes and released new annotated datasets. Ritter et al. (2011) added new tags for Twitter specific phenomena such as #hashtags and @usernames. Gimpel et al. (2011), developed a POS tagset specifically for English Twitter and a new dataset of manually tagged tweets. Owoputi et al. (2013) released a new manually annotated dataset for English Twitter POS tagging along with a part of speech tagger for online conversational text. There have also been efforts on POS tagging for other languages such as Irish (Lynn et al., 2015) and Italian (Bosco et al., 2016). A shared task on the Automatic Linguistic Annotation of Computer-Mediated Communication (CMC) and Web Corpora for German was also organized by Beißwenger et al. (2016) to observe whether both CMC and Web corpora can be processed using the same methodologies and whether improved models can be introduced for tokenization and POS tagging of German computer-mediated communication using the new annotated data and other techniques, such as domain adaptation. Domain adaptation and regularization are helpful techniques when dealing with low-resource text types and many studies have focused on enhancing POS tagging using such methods (Meftah et al., 2019; März et al., 2019).

Some studies have conducted error analysis of social media taggers, though not yet on Reddit. Derczynski et al. (2013) evaluated the performance of existing POS taggers on Twitter datasets. They also provide an in-depth analysis of the errors on the tokens that were not seen during training. They report gold standard error, slang, genre specific tokens and unseen proper nouns among the common error categories. Albogamy and Ramsay (2016) also evaluate state-of-the-art POS taggers on Arabic tweets. They categorize errors into 2 groups: errors on Arabic words and errors on non-Arabic tokens. Each of these groups includes subcategories such as named entities that were not seen during training, concatenation of multiple words, emoticons, foreign words, and others.

To the best of our knowledge, such in-depth studies have not yet been done on Reddit even though it is widely used as a data source for different NLP tasks. In this paper, we study genre effects on POS tagging accuracy for Reddit text when training data itself comes entirely from the Web (but not from Reddit), from other large benchmark resources such as OntoNotes (Hovy et al., 2006)) or both. We provide a detailed error analysis of different models, which suggests that some of the difficulties in tagging Reddit are not only due to the noisy nature of text online, but also to specific language use in Reddit as a genre. We also present an ensemble tagging approach that has a higher accuracy than the best single training genre baseline.

3. Approach

3.1. Data

In this study, we use three different corpora with different genres. The main corpus we used is GUM (the Georgetown University Multilayer corpus (Zeldes, 2017)) which was chosen because it contains gold standard tagged Reddit data. The corpus has manual annotation for different tasks such as POS tagging, lemmatization, dependency parses, discourse parses and entity and coreference resolution (Zeldes, 2017), though the latter layers are not used in this study. Currently, GUM comprises about 130,000 tokens with data from 8 different genres in English, which, aside from Reddit, include creative commons licensed Academic papers and Fiction, Biographies (Bio) from Wikipedia, WikiNews Interviews and News stories, Wikivoyage travel guides and Wikihow how-to guides (Whow). Importantly, all of the data in the corpus was harvested from the Web, meaning that even when training on other genres and testing on Reddit, only data which is encountered on the Internet is involved. In order to get comparable numbers for models trained on other popular benchmark resources, we also use larger corpora such as EWT (Bies et al., 2012) (about 250,000 tokens of data from the Web) and English OntoNotes (Weischedel et al., 2013) (about 2.6 million tokens, mostly from edited print texts and spoken data) in our experiments which are mainly used for POS tagging evaluations.

We have 12 different training splits for this task; for every GUM genre except for Reddit, we use all available data as the training set. Reddit has the smallest training set since we need some of the documents for development and test sets. Out of 11,182 annotated Reddit tokens in GUM version 5, we use 5,727 tokens for training, and 2,489 tokens for development and 2,966 tokens for the test set. The Reddit documents are from different discussion threads which makes evaluation more realistic.

We also create a split that contains the training data of multiple genres (Reddit, Academic, Bio, Fiction, Interview, News, Voyage, Whow) (*Multiple Genres*) and another one which contains training data from the same genres except for Reddit (*Multiple Genres w/o Reddit*). The size of all these training sets is shown in Table 1. For all of our models, we use the same Reddit development and test sets mentioned above.

For OntoNotes and EWT we use the entire corpora as datasets, without considering sub-genres within those resources, as most papers using them for training employ the entire corpus training set without internal distinctions. Although we recognize it would be interesting to analyze the contents of these data sets further, we leave that task open for future studies.

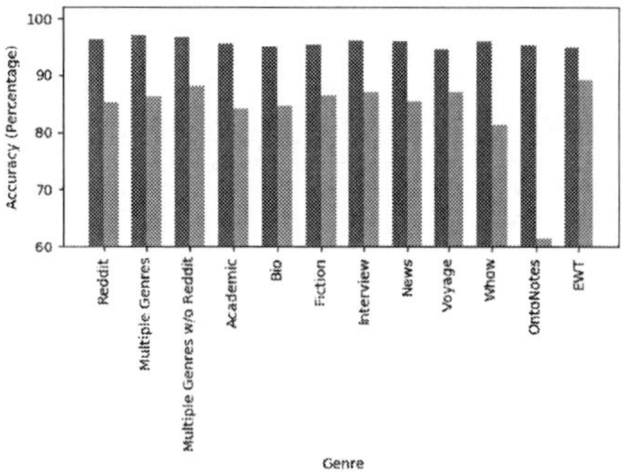

Figure 1: Accuracy on *Known* and *Unknown* tokens per genre; blue bars (left) correspond to accuracy of Known tokens and orange bars (right) correspond to accuracy of Unknown tokens.

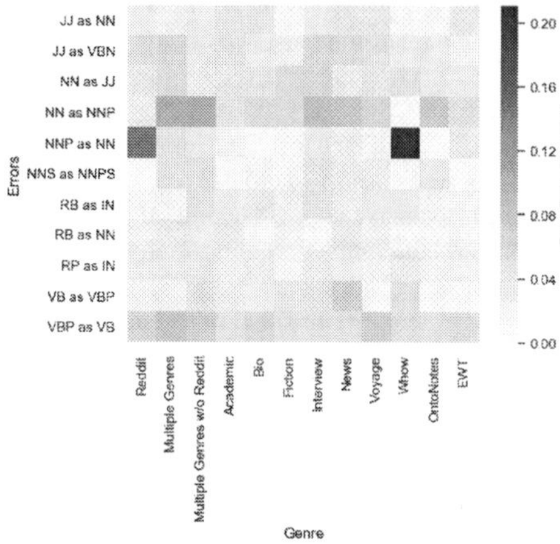

Figure 2: Most common prediction errors on the test set across models trained on different genres. Y-axis labeling: *A as B* means A incorrectly tagged as B.

3.2. Tagger

For tagging, we choose a state-of-the-art neural sequence tagger, Flair (Akbik et al., 2018) and retrain it on our splits. We used the sequence tagger model with the default 256 hidden unit bi-directional LSTM and trained with contextualized pre-trained Flair embeddings and uncontextualized pre-trained character embeddings, then evaluated performance by accuracy per token and also full-sentence accuracy (proportion of perfectly tagged sentences), since "a single bad mistake in a sentence can greatly throw off the usefulness of a tagger to downstream tasks such as dependency parsing" (Manning, 2011).

Finally, we use an ensemble approach to combine results from multiple models and study how much each of these sources contributes to the results of the ensemble model [1]. We use all the retrained Flair models on single genres except *Reddit*, and then make predictions on the Reddit training set. We then use these predictions as training features for our ensemble model, which uses XGBoost as a meta-learner. Based on the analysis described in section 4 and to help the model better distinguish between NN and NNP, we also incorporate three other features to help the ensemble classifier; for each token, we check if 1) the token itself, 2) the lower-cased version of the token and 3) the token starting with a capital letter, exists in a knowledge base taken from (Zeldes and Zhang, 2016) and add any entity types (e.g. Person, Organization etc.) which this token might have as n-hot encoded features. We then evaluate the classifier on the Reddit test set and perform an ablation study by removing the predictions of each genre and observing the changes in the accuracy.

4. Results and Analysis

The results of our experiments are shown in Table 1. As expected, the highest per token and also full-sentence accuracy belong to the model trained on multiple genres since there is more training data available and we are also including in-domain Reddit data in training. The model trained on multiple genres without Reddit gets only slightly lower accuracy per token, however, we observe a 3.2% drop on full-sentence accuracy. Even though the Reddit model has the smallest amount of data for training (less than half of most other genres, due to the held out dev and test sets), it performs better than almost all models trained on different genres, which shows the high importance of even a small amount of in-domain data. Interestingly, the model trained on interviews works slightly better than the model trained on Reddit, probably because interviews published online are the most similar to the largely first and second person interactions found in Reddit forum discussions, and because the interview dataset is substantially larger than the Reddit training data.

In Table 2, we can compare errors made by different models on the same sentences. None of the models can predict correct POS tags for the whole sentences. Surprisingly, even though *Multiple Genres* has more data than *Multiple Genres w/o Reddit* including in-domain data, it performs worse in the first sentence; it cannot predict the tag NNP for the token 'Wild'.

The most common error among all of the models is mistagging the token 'b.' in the first sentence, which is indicating an item of a list and should get the tag LS. The second most common mistake seems to be the emoticon :) in the second sentence. Reddit and EWT are the only models predicting correct tags for this token. 'love' has the gold label VBP but it is predicted as VB or NN by different models, due to the low frequency of subjectless sentences, which resemble imperatives or fragments if the missing 'I' is not recognized. NNP tokens such as 'Boo' or 'Wild' are incorrectly tagged as NN by many of the models, mirroring findings on NNP tagging problems in previous studies.

We also look at the accuracy of models on *Unknown* tokens (not seen during training) and *Known* tokens separately. Figure 1 shows these results. Except for models trained on Academic, Bio, Whow and OntoNotes data, all other models perform better than the Reddit model on Un-

[1]Setup details are available at `https://github.com/shabnam-b/reddit-pos-ensemble.git`

	Reddit	**Multiple Genres**	**Multiple Genres w/o Reddit**	**Academic**	**Bio**	**Fiction**
Training Set Size (Tokens)	5,727	107,004	101,277	11,868	12,562	12,843
Per Token	93.53	**95.89**	95.72	91.81	91.77	93.29
Full-sentence	36.08	**53.16**	49.37	29.75	25.32	37.97

	Interview	**News**	**Voyage**	**Whow**	**OntoNotes**	**EWT**
Training Set Size (Tokens)	18,037	14,092	14,955	16,920	2,442,000	204,609
Per Token	94.23	93.26	92.48	92.95	93.73	94.81
Full-sentence	39.87	31.01	30.38	31.01	41.14	48.10

Table 1: Accuracy scores calculated for tokens and full-sentences when trained on different genres individually and tested on Reddit.

Model	**Example**
Reddit	*b./: Using these to release Boo/NN into "The Wild/NN"* *love/VB when I see people/places from Austin on FN :)*
Multiple Genres	*b./FW Using these to release Boo/NN into "The Wild/NN"* *love/VB when I see people/places from Austin on FN :)/-RRB-*
Multiple Genres w/o Reddit	*b./FW Using these to release Boo/NN into "The Wild"* *love/VB when I see people/places from Austin on FN :)/:*
Academic	*b./NN Using these to release Boo into "/DT The Wild"/CC* *love/NN when I see people/places from Austin on FN :)/:*
Bio	*b./FW Using these to release Boo into "The Wild"* *love/NN when I see people //CC places from Austin on FN :)/:*
Fiction	*b./" Using these to release Boo into "/NNP The Wild"* *love/NN when I see people //: places from Austin on FN :)/:*
Interview	*b./: Using these to release Boo into "The/NNP Wild"* *love/VB when I see people //CC places from Austin on FN :)/:*
News	*b./NNP Using these to release Boo/NN into "The Wild"* *love/NN when I see people/places from Austin on FN :)/:*
Voyage	*b./RB Using these to release Boo/NN into "The Wild"* *love/VB when I see people/places from Austin on FN :)/:*
Whow	*b./: Using these to release Boo/NN into "The Wild/NN"* *love/VB when I see people/places from Austin on FN :)/:*
OntoNotes	*b./NN Using these to release Boo into "The Wild"* *love/VB when I see people/places from Austin on FN :)/.*
EWT	*b./RB Using these to release Boo/NN into "The Wild"* *love/VB when I see people//,places from Austin on FN :)*

Table 2: Errors made by different models on two example sentences from Reddit posts.

known tokens, but this again could be the result of Reddit having a very small training set compared to other genres.

To further analyze the results, we looked at misclassifications which were common among multiple genres. The results are shown in Figure 2. The most common errors across all genres are VBP predicted as VB and NN predicted as NNP. The latter can stem from looser capitalization distinctions online, while the former can result when subject pronouns are dropped in informal English (e.g. 'want to come?' or 'need this right now'). Comparing *Multiple Genres* and *Multiple Genres w/o Reddit*, we can observe that adding the Reddit data results in more accurate RB, RP, and VB tagging. We can also observe that a huge proportion of the *Whow* model's errors belongs to mistagging NNP as NN, which is probably the result of fewer proper nouns appearing in Wikihow articles since they are sets of instructions for various tasks.

Furthermore, we manually observed 50 of the errors that the *Multiple Genres w/o Reddit* model made. The most common errors were 1) *Emoticons:* Emoticons such as :) , :(or others which are gold labeled as SYM are labeled with different tags such as ", : or even NNP in cases where they contain an alphabetical character such as in D:>. 2) *Interjections* and mostly swear words appear in social media text more than other genres, as well as phonetic elongation or representations with repeated characters such as 'NANANANA', which do not appear in formal written text, but are common among users in social media (Sanguinetti et al., 2020). Some of these tokens were tagged as NNP instead of gold standard UH. Some other errors were 3) *Proper nouns not starting with a capital letter* (e.g. bobby/NN), 4) *Foreign words* (e.g. etcetera/NNP) and 5) *Abbreviations* (e.g. BTW/NNP).

Finally, in order to harness the increased stability offered by consulting multiple models and different features, Table 3 shows the results of the ensemble model described in Section 3. Except for Interview, all models positively contribute to the overall accuracy. Only the Interview model's

Model	Per Token	Full-sentence
StanfordNLP	94.81	46.84
TreeTagger	92.08	28.48
Ensemble	95.99	53.80
- (Academic)	95.92	53.80
- (Bio)	95.89	53.16
- (Fiction)	95.95	54.43
- (Interview)	**96.12**	**56.96**
- (News)	95.89	53.80
- (Voyage)	95.92	55.06
- (Whow)	95.82	51.90
- (OntoNotes)	95.55	50.00
- (EWT)	95.62	50.63

Table 3: Accuracy score of StanfordNLP, TreeTagger and ensemble XGBoost when using the prediction of all trained models, and when each model is removed.

removal from the ensemble improves upon the results in Table 1 both in terms of per token accuracy and full sentence accuracy, which suggests that, at least for the test set at hand, other genres combined do a better job of predicting correct tags, despite the usefulness of interviews in a single genre model. The final model without 'interview' thus represents our best results and a new state-of-the-art score on Reddit tagging using the GUM benchmark, with 96.12% accuracy despite not including any Reddit data in training the features for the meta-classifier. Furthermore, we compare these results with two pretrained off-the-shelf taggers: TreeTagger trained on Penn treebank and StanfordNLP (Qi et al., 2018) trained on GUM. We also looked at the effect of removing the named entity features on the results; without the named entities, the best model's accuracy (Ensemble-Interview) drops to 95.89% per token and 55.06% for full-sentence. Comparing these numbers to the best single model in Table 1, the ensemble approach without any extra features is resulting in the same token accuracy, but we get almost 2% increase in full-sentence accuracy.

5. Conclusion

In this work, we looked at the effect of genre on Reddit POS tagging. We analyzed the results of the same tagger, trained on 10 different sources with multiple genres, including Reddit itself, and also trained on the combination of all genres. We observed that within single genre models, the Interview model has the highest accuracy on Reddit, which might be the result of comparatively much training data (Interview has somewhat more tokens than the other single genre datasets), or the nature of some of the Reddit documents which are back and forth conversations between different users and is similar to the nature of interviews. However, in combination with other models in the ensemble approach, removing the Interview model seemed to increase the performance slightly, and OntoNotes predictions seem to have the most positive contributions to the accuracy of the ensemble model, possibly because of the wide coverage of rare items resulting from the large corpus size. Finally, the results of our error analysis were in line with prior studies on Web text-types other than Reddit. The most important problem in this task using deep learning models with word/character embeddings is when we have unseen data in the test set; this unseen data could be in the form of creative emoticons, repeated characters in a word, abbreviations, etc. To improve the performance on user-generated content in domains such as social media, we either need to collect sufficient in-domain data to train a genre-specific model, or find other ways of addressing unseen tokens such as using lexical resources or doing specific preprocessing to normalize the tokens before testing. The present paper demonstrates that, in the absence of substantial amounts of in-domain data, ensembling the outputs of multiple tagging models with different training datasets can lead to very good results, in this case giving a new SOA score of 96.12% token accuracy on the Reddit data. At the same time, full-sentence accuracy remains below 57%, suggesting that there is still room for substantial improvements.

6. Bibliographical References

Akbik, A., Blythe, D., and Vollgraf, R. (2018). Contextual string embeddings for sequence labeling. In *Proceedings of the 27th International Conference on Computational Linguistics*, pages 1638–1649, Santa Fe, New Mexico, USA, August. Association for Computational Linguistics.

Albogamy, F. and Ramsay, A. (2016). Fast and robust POS tagger for Arabic tweets using agreement-based bootstrapping. In *Proceedings of the Tenth International Conference on Language Resources and Evaluation (LREC 2016)*, pages 1500–1506, Portorož, Slovenia, May. European Language Resources Association (ELRA).

Beißwenger, M., Bartsch, S., Evert, S., and Würzner, K.-M. (2016). EmpiriST 2015: A shared task on the automatic linguistic annotation of computer-mediated communication and web corpora. In *Proceedings of the 10th Web as Corpus Workshop*, pages 44–56, Berlin, August. Association for Computational Linguistics.

Bosco, C., Fabio, T., Andrea, B., and Mazzei, A. (2016). Overview of the evalita 2016 part of speech on twitter for italian task. In *Fifth Evaluation Campaign of Natural Language Processing and Speech Tools for Italian. Final Workshop (EVALITA 2016)*, volume 1749.

Choi, J. D. (2016). Dynamic feature induction: The last gist to the state-of-the-art. In *Proceedings of the 2016 Conference of the North American Chapter of the Association for Computational Linguistics: Human Language Technologies*, pages 271–281, San Diego, California, June. Association for Computational Linguistics.

Derczynski, L., Ritter, A., Clark, S., and Bontcheva, K. (2013). Twitter part-of-speech tagging for all: Overcoming sparse and noisy data. In *Proceedings of the International Conference Recent Advances in Natural Language Processing RANLP 2013*, pages 198–206, Hissar, Bulgaria, September. INCOMA Ltd. Shoumen, BULGARIA.

Foster, J., Cetinoglu, O., Wagner, J., Le Roux, J., Hogan, S., Nivre, J., Hogan, D., and Van Genabith, J. (2011). # hardtoparse: POS tagging and parsing the Twitterverse.

In *Workshops at the Twenty-Fifth AAAI Conference on Artificial Intelligence*.

Giesbrecht, E. and Evert, S. (2009). Is part-of-speech tagging a solved task? an evaluation of pos taggers for the german web as corpus. In *Proceedings of the 5th Web as Corpus Workshop*.

Gimpel, K., Schneider, N., O'Connor, B., Das, D., Mills, D., Eisenstein, J., Heilman, M., Yogatama, D., Flanigan, J., and Smith, N. A. (2011). Part-of-speech tagging for twitter: Annotation, features, and experiments. In *Proceedings of the 49th Annual Meeting of the Association for Computational Linguistics: Human Language Technologies*, pages 42–47, Portland, Oregon, USA, June. Association for Computational Linguistics.

Gui, T., Zhang, Q., Huang, H., Peng, M., and Huang, X. (2017). Part-of-speech tagging for twitter with adversarial neural networks. In *Proceedings of the 2017 Conference on Empirical Methods in Natural Language Processing*, pages 2411–2420, Copenhagen, Denmark, September. Association for Computational Linguistics.

Hovy, E., Marcus, M., Palmer, M., Ramshaw, L., and Weischedel, R. (2006). OntoNotes: The 90% solution. In *Proceedings of the Human Language Technology Conference of the NAACL, Companion Volume: Short Papers*, pages 57–60, New York.

Huang, Z., Xu, W., and Yu, K. (2015). Bidirectional lstm-crf models for sequence tagging. *arXiv preprint arXiv:1508.01991*.

Liu, Y., Zhu, Y., Che, W., Qin, B., Schneider, N., and Smith, N. A. (2018). Parsing tweets into universal dependencies. In *Proceedings of the 2018 Conference of the North American Chapter of the Association for Computational Linguistics: Human Language Technologies, Volume 1 (Long Papers)*, pages 965–975, New Orleans, Louisiana, June. Association for Computational Linguistics.

Lynn, T., Scannell, K., and Maguire, E. (2015). Minority language twitter: Part-of-speech tagging and analysis of Irish tweets. In *Proceedings of the Workshop on Noisy User-generated Text*, pages 1–8, Beijing, China, July. Association for Computational Linguistics.

Manning, C. D. (2011). Part-of-speech tagging from 97% to 100%: is it time for some linguistics? In *International conference on intelligent text processing and computational linguistics*, pages 171–189. Springer.

März, L., Trautmann, D., and Roth, B. (2019). Domain adaptation for part-of-speech tagging of noisy user-generated text. In *Proceedings of the 2019 Conference of the North American Chapter of the Association for Computational Linguistics: Human Language Technologies, Volume 1 (Long and Short Papers)*, pages 3415–3420, Minneapolis, Minnesota, June. Association for Computational Linguistics.

Meftah, S. and Semmar, N. (2018). A neural network model for part-of-speech tagging of social media texts. In *Proceedings of the Eleventh International Conference on Language Resources and Evaluation (LREC-2018)*, Miyazaki, Japan, May. European Languages Resources Association (ELRA).

Meftah, S., Tamaazousti, Y., Semmar, N., Essafi, H., and Sadat, F. (2019). Joint learning of pre-trained and random units for domain adaptation in part-of-speech tagging. In *Proceedings of the 2019 Conference of the North American Chapter of the Association for Computational Linguistics: Human Language Technologies, Volume 1 (Long and Short Papers)*, pages 4107–4112, Minneapolis, Minnesota, June. Association for Computational Linguistics.

Mueller, T., Schmid, H., and Schütze, H. (2013). Efficient higher-order CRFs for morphological tagging. In *Proceedings of the 2013 Conference on Empirical Methods in Natural Language Processing*, pages 322–332, Seattle, Washington, USA, October. Association for Computational Linguistics.

Neunerdt, M., Trevisan, B., Reyer, M., and Mathar, R. (2013). Part-of-speech tagging for social media texts. In *Language Processing and Knowledge in the Web*, pages 139–150. Springer.

Owoputi, O., O'Connor, B., Dyer, C., Gimpel, K., Schneider, N., and Smith, N. A. (2013). Improved part-of-speech tagging for online conversational text with word clusters. In *Proceedings of the 2013 Conference of the North American Chapter of the Association for Computational Linguistics: Human Language Technologies*, pages 380–390, Atlanta, Georgia, June. Association for Computational Linguistics.

Qi, P., Dozat, T., Zhang, Y., and Manning, C. D. (2018). Universal dependency parsing from scratch. In *Proceedings of the CoNLL 2018 Shared Task: Multilingual Parsing from Raw Text to Universal Dependencies*, pages 160–170, Brussels, Belgium. Association for Computational Linguistics.

Ritter, A., Clark, S., Mausam, and Etzioni, O. (2011). Named entity recognition in tweets: An experimental study. In *Proceedings of the 2011 Conference on Empirical Methods in Natural Language Processing*, pages 1524–1534, Edinburgh, Scotland, UK., July. Association for Computational Linguistics.

Sanguinetti, M., Bosco, C., Cassidy, L., Özlem Çetinoğlu, Cignarella, A. T., Lynn, T., Rehbein, I., Ruppenhofer, J., Seddah, D., and Zeldes, A. (2020). Treebanking user-generated content: A proposal for a unified representation in universal dependencies. In *Proceedings of LREC 2020*, Marseille, France.

Sun, X. (2014). Structure regularization for structured prediction. In *Advances in Neural Information Processing Systems 27*, pages 2402–2410. Curran Associates, Inc.

Zeldes, A. and Zhang, S. (2016). When annotation schemes change rules help: A configurable approach to coreference resolution beyond OntoNotes. In *Proceedings of the NAACL2016 Workshop on Coreference Resolution Beyond OntoNotes (CORBON)*, pages 92–101, San Diego, CA.

Zeldes, A. (2017). The GUM corpus: Creating multilayer resources in the classroom. *Language Resources and Evaluation*, 51(3):581–612.

7. Language Resource References

Ann Bies and Justin Mott and Colin Warner and Seth Kulick. (2012). *English Web Treebank*. LDC, ISLRN

230-396-178-102-3.

Ralph Weischedel and Martha Palmer and Mitchell Marcus and Eduard Hovy and Sameer Pradhan and Lance Ramshaw and Nianwen Xue and Ann Taylor and Jeff Kaufman and Michelle Franchini and Mohammed El-Bachouti and Robert Belvin and Ann Houston. (2013). *OntoNotes Release 5.0.* LDC, 5.0, ISLRN 151-738-649-048-2.

Amir Zeldes. (2017). *The Georgetown University Multilayer Corpus.* Georgetown University.

Proceedings of the 12th Web as Corpus Workshop, pages 57–64
Language Resources and Evaluation Conference (LREC 2020), Marseille, 11–16 May 2020

Streaming Language-Specific Twitter Data with Optimal Keywords

Tim, Kreutz, Walter, Daelemans
CLiPS, University of Antwerp
Prinsstraat 13, 2000 Antwerp, Belgium
tim.kreutz, walter.daelemans@uantwerpen.be

Abstract

The Twitter Streaming API has been used to create language-specific corpora with varying degrees of success. Selecting a filter of frequent yet distinct keywords for German resulted in a near-complete collection of German tweets. This method is promising as it keeps within Twitter endpoint limitations and could be applied to other languages besides German. But so far no research has compared methods for selecting optimal keywords for this task. This paper proposes a method for finding optimal key phrases based on a greedy solution to the maximum coverage problem. We generate candidate key phrases for the 50 most frequent languages on Twitter. Candidates are then iteratively selected based on a variety of scoring functions applied to their coverage of target tweets. Selecting candidates based on the scoring function that exponentiates the precision of a key phrase and weighs it by recall achieved the best results overall. Some target languages yield lower results than what could be expected from their prevalence on Twitter. Upon analyzing the errors, we find that these are languages that are very close to more prevalent languages. In these cases, key phrases that limit finding the competitive language are selected, and overall recall on the target language also decreases. We publish the resulting optimized lists for each language as a resource. The code to generate lists for other research objectives is also supplied.

Keywords: twitter, social media, data collection, corpus linguistics

1. Introduction

Twitter data has frequently been used to study the public reaction to specific topics or events (Leetaru et al., 2013). In Natural Language Processing this trend is mirrored in popular subtasks like sentiment mining and event detection, and the appeal of tweets for these purposes is understandable; they comprise abundant, open and mostly unfiltered public feedback (Barnaghi et al., 2016).

But collecting tweets for diverse purposes is no straightforward task. Researchers ultimately make design choices on which keywords, hashtags and users to search, without any gold standard reference to test the resulting data snapshot. Additionally, not all tweets are made available to the search index (Twitter, 2019c). Twitter is free to put any restrictions on their results, whether it is on the maximum number of hits or on how far back search results go.

As an alternative to the retrospective search approach, the Twitter Streaming API (Twitter, 2019b) has been used to collect high-volume language-specific corpora in real-time. By filtering the stream on a list of frequent yet distinct keywords for a specific language, it is possible to achieve high coverage of a reference set. Such lists of keywords have been created for Dutch (Tjong Kim Sang and Van den Bosch, 2013), Italian (Basile and Nissim, 2013), German (Scheffler, 2014), Hindi, Telugu and Bengali (Choudhary et al., 2018).

This paper offers three main improvements to the previous work. First, we compare methods for selecting optimal keywords for creating language-specific Twitter corpora. Second, we closely replicate the real-world performance of these methods in our experimental setup so that the limitations of the resulting corpora are known for any downstream task. Third, although we conform to the Twitter Developer Agreement (Twitter, 2019a) and will not share the language-specific corpora, we do provide the lists of optimized keywords for the top 50 languages on Twitter and the code to generate lists for other languages.

2. Background

Distribution of large collections of tweets is disallowed under the Twitter Developer Agreement and Policy (Twitter, 2019a). Initiatives to share large general-purpose Twitter collection, such as the Edinburgh Twitter Corpus (Petrović et al., 2010) have been shut down under this regulation.

Consequently, studies on Twitter data have moved away from large scale general-purpose collections to data snapshots designed for a specific downstream task. Three main filtering approaches can be distinguished in previous work.

2.1. Location-based Filtering

Twitter introduced an opt-in for sending location information with tweets in 2009. This has allowed researchers to study language use alongside fine-grained geographic distinctions.

Location-based filtering has proven invaluable for creating datasets for dialectology with relatively low effort (Eisenstein et al., 2010; Huang et al., 2016). Laitinen et al. (2018) show that location-based filtering can successfully be deployed for studying language spread across country borders.

Location-based filtering is less suitable for creating language-specific corpora. Bergsma et al. (2012) design filters based on the coordinates of major cities where speakers of a target language are prominent. The resulting collections were relatively pure for Arabic (99.9%) and Farsi (99.7%) but not for Urdu (61.0%). Since a very low percentage (between 0.7% and 2.9% depending on the country) of Twitter users enable location sharing, filtering by location yields very low coverage (Barbaresi, 2016).

2.2. User-based Filtering

Filtering by username is useful in cases where a very specific group of users is targeted. Praet et al. (2018) collected tweets by Flemish politicians to analyze which political issues were most often communicated, and whether

this aligned with their parties' agenda.
Barbaresi (2016) used user-based filtering in conjunction with location-based filtering to find tweets by Austrian Twitter users. The resulting collection had mostly English (42.2%) language tweets.

2.3. Word-based Filtering

Word-based filtering best suits the purpose of creating language-specific corpora. Scheffler (2014) was able to collect a near-complete snapshot of German twitter messages by tapping the Streaming API for German stopwords. They removed words from the list that are also frequent in other languages (such as 'war' and 'die' for English) and extended it with other frequent and distinctive German words. To test for coverage, the collection obtained through word-based filtering was compared to collections retrieved with location-based and user-based filtering during the same time period. Only around 5% of German tweets was missing from the collection obtained through word-based filtering.
Handpicked lists of filter words were also used for collecting Dutch tweets (Tjong Kim Sang and Van den Bosch, 2013). The authors add Twitter-specific terms, such as trending Dutch hashtags, to their keywords but report that a lot of other-language tweets still slip through the filter.
A more systematic approach can be found in Basile and Nissim (2013). Cross-language homographs were detected using Google Ngrams and removed from a list of most frequent Italian words. Using only the top 20 of the remaining terms yielded enough data for the eventual purpose of creating an Italian corpus for sentiment analysis.

2.4. Toward Optimal Filtering

Previous work on word-based filtering has mostly been deployed as an intermediate step for a downstream task. These papers understandably deploy some heuristic method of selecting keywords, and usually do not compare the resulting snapshot with a reference set.
Kreutz and Daelemans (2019) instead focus solely on obtaining optimized keywords. Their list of optimized keywords for Dutch outperforms the hand-picked list in Tjong Kim Sang and Van den Bosch (2013) in both precision and recall. From intrinsic evaluation it is also clear that the optimized list benefits from being generated on the domain it is trying to retrieve.
We extend the work of Kreutz and Daelemans (2019) by comparing additional optimization methods and applying these to languages other than Dutch. In the process of developing optimal lists that can be used to collect language-specific Twitter corpora for the 50 most common languages on Twitter, we provide the statistics that can be cited as limitations for these collections.

3. Data

To generate optimal keywords over Twitter data, we design an experimental setup that mirrors the performance of the keywords on the real-time stream.

3.1. Twitter API Constraints

The Twitter API imposes a 1% rate limit, and will automatically sample down to the rate limit when more tweets pass the filter (Twitter, 2019b). This puts a hard limit on the number of tweets that can be obtained for the more dominant languages on Twitter. Language prevalence can be used to determine the maximum coverage any filtering can achieve.

3.2. Language Prevalence

We collected tweets using the Twitter sprinkler (Twitter, 2019b) over a period of six months from October 2017 to March 2018. The Twitter Sprinkler is an access point of the Twitter Streaming API that can yield 1% of all tweets at any time. Filtering of the complete datastream can be done by giving keyphrases, geo-locations, or user handles. We did not apply any filtering to best approximate a random sample. This resulted in roughly 570 million tweets.
Although Twitter predicts its own IETF language tags for most tweets, we found on initial inspection that a pre-trained FastText language identification model (Joulin et al., 2017) identified a larger part of the tweets. We think it is key to assign labels to difficult and even code mixed tweets. These non-trivial cases crop up in the real-world setting and cannot be ignored for generating keyphrases and for reporting their performance.
The FastText (large) 176 ISO-tag model was used to assign silver labels to each tweet. The tags come from a combination of the ISO 639-1 and ISO 639-2 standards found on the FastText website (Grave, 2017). Table 1 shows the language prevalence of the five most and the five least identified languages. FREQ is the relative frequency over our entire dataset. MEAN is the relative frequency averaged per hour and better reflects language prevalence normalised over time. MEAN can be used to determine how many tweets cannot be retrieved due to the 1% rate limit. MAX shows the maximum hourly relative frequency. Languages that never surpass the 1% rate limit throughout the day can theoretically be collected in full.

Language	FREQ	MEAN	MAX
1. English	39.06%	39.21%	46.93%
2. Japanese	19.18%	19.09%	29.64%
3. Spanish	9.52%	9.45%	13.27%
4. Arabic	7.29%	7.39%	10.82%
5. Portuguese	5.17%	5.10%	9.59%
<40 more languages>			
46. Azerbaijani	0.01%	0.01%	0.02%
47. Marathi	0.01%	0.01%	0.02%
48. Guarani	0.01%	0.01%	0.02%
49. Albanian	0.01%	0.01%	0.01%
50. Kannada	0.01%	0.01%	0.01%

Table 1: Language frequency (FREQ), averaged frequency per hour (MEAN) and maximum average frequency per hour (MAX) for the most and least identified languages in 6 months of Twitter data.

The Table 1 rankings partially correspond to earlier analyses of the language composition of Twitter. Two notable differences are the increase in the number of Arabic tweets, and a decline in English language tweets compared to a

2011 study (Hong et al., 2011). We expect these differences to be due to increased popularity of Twitter in Arabic countries while the U.S. user base stagnated (Semiocast, 2011; Bloomberg, 2019). However, differences can also be due to the FastText model identifying more tweets (roughly 9%) than the IETF labels used in Hong et al. (2011).

3.3. Experimental Setup

After removing retweets, 10,000 tweets were sampled for the 50 most frequent languages. Non-target language tweets were added conform to the language distributions. For example, since Spanish tweets represent roughly 9.52% of the stream, we sampled 105,042 ($\frac{10000}{0.0952}$) other-language tweets. Since more infrequent languages greatly inflate the number of other-language tweets supplemented in their dataset, we opted for a cut-off after the 50 most frequent languages.

We created development and test data in a similar way, by sampling roughly 5,000 target language tweets and adding other language tweets based on their distribution.

While creating separate data sets for each of the targeted languages may seem extraneous, we opted for this approach because it would guarantee that key phrase lists would be sampled from roughly the same number of tweets for each language. This way, the quality of key phrases can never be attributed to differences in data size.

3.4. Preprocessing

In preparation of generating and testing keywords, tweets are parsed according to Twitter documentation (Twitter, 2019a). Tweets were lowercased and any punctuation except @ (for mentions of other users) and # (for hashtag topic markers) were removed.

4. Methods

The Twitter API allows an input of up to 400 60-byte strings. Disjunctive search is performed between the 400 inputs, and any tweet matching the conjunctive presence of tokens in an input is retrieved (Twitter, 2019a). From now on, string inputs will be referred to as *key phrases*.

We generate token *powersets*; exhaustive combinations of tokens present in the target language tweets. The notion is that each token combination generated from a tweet can be used as a key phrase to retrieve that tweet from the stream. Each key phrase is thus associated with a set of target- and other-language tweets, and in extension a recall and precision score.

4.1. Maximum Coverage of Tweets

Optimal key phrases maximally cover the set of target language tweets, whilst limiting the number of other-language tweets retrieved. The latter consideration is especially important considering the 1% rate limit. Key phrases that confuse target language tweets with other (dominant) languages can lead to results that are not only impure, but also incomplete due to down-sampling.

Formally, we consider a collection of key phrases K, generated from a target language l, $K^l = \{K^l_1, K^l_2, ..., K^l_n\}$ and a parallel collection T of sets of tweets identified by those phrases, $T = \{T_1, T_2, ..., T_n\}$. We compare algorithms for selecting up to 400 phrases from K to optimize a variety of objectives to target set T^l.

Input : $K; T$;
Output: Optimized key phrases O

Function `Optimal` (K, T) **:**
    $bestscore \leftarrow 0$
    $bestphrase \leftarrow None$
    for $i \leftarrow 0$ **to** $|K|$ **do**
        if `Score` $(T_i) > bestscore$ **then**
            $bestscore \leftarrow$ `Score` (T_i).
            $bestphrase \leftarrow K_i$.
    return $bestphrase$

Function `Run` $(K, T, n \leftarrow 400)$ **:**
    $O \leftarrow \varnothing$
    for $i \leftarrow 0$ **to** n **do**
        Remove tweets covered by O from every set in T.
        Add `Optimal` (K, T) to O.
    return O

Figure 1: Our method iteratively picks a phrase K_i with the highest score with regards to target set T_l and removes all retrieved tweets from the remaining items in T.

4.2. Scoring Functions

In its classic setting a maximum coverage problem optimizes recall over a target set. Since we also care about precision, we design scoring functions to reflect this objective alongside the naive optimization of recall and precision:

1. Optimize Recall (R)
2. Optimize Precision (P)
3. Optimize Recall, but ensure a precision threshold of .9 for each phrase (R_p)
4. Optimize Precision, but ensure a recall threshold of .01 for each phrase (P_r)
5. Weight Precision$^\beta$ by Recall. Higher β adds more importance to precision ($P^\beta * R$)

Although F-score seems like another likely candidate for scoring key phrases, its reliance on a balanced recall and precision, even in adaptations like F-beta where precision receives more weight, make it unsuitable. We demonstrate the pitfall of reliance on recall sufficiently with scoring functions 1 and 4.

4.3. Greedy Selection

We consider only a greedy approach to selecting key phrases, due to the huge number of candidates. Greedy optimization of maximum coverage problems is shown to be the best approximation algorithm in polynomial time (Feige, 1998). The greedy algorithm iteratively picks a key phrase according to a scoring function from the preceding list. The covered tweets are then removed and scores are recalculated before picking the next phrase (Figure 1).

4.4. Baselines

Naive scoring functions 1 and 2 can be expected to perform poorly for the task of creating language-specific Twitter corpora. We expect optimization over recall to select the stopwords that best identify a target language in addition to other generic terms such as partial URLs. Optimizing precision conversely can yield some terms occurring in only a few tweets.

For more reasonable baseline behavior we draw from previous work in word-based filtering of tweets in Section 2.3. First, keyword lists are compiled from the 400 most frequent tokens in a target language training set in line with Choudhary et al. (2018). These lists are then filtered for cross-language homographs for the second baseline. However, making corrections for each language by hand as seen for Dutch (Tjong Kim Sang and Van den Bosch, 2013) and German (Scheffler, 2014) would require significant language expertise and time investment. We instead assure that none of the 400 selected words are present in the 1000 most frequent terms of non-target languages. This automatic filtering of frequent terms is comparable to what has been done for Italian (Basile and Nissim, 2013).

5. Results

In this section we first qualitatively analyze the key phrases selected by the different scoring functions. Some expected drawbacks of each of the greedy selection approaches have been formulated in the previous section, and are tested by manual inspection.

We do not assume that scoring functions perform uniformly for each target language. Specifically, we expect a prevalence effect whereby language that are more common on Twitter would benefit from higher precision phrases as confusion with other languages is more costly. False positives fill up the stream permitted by the Twitter rate limit and would lower overall performance. For rarer languages, this is less important. The $P^{\beta} * R$ scoring function will be grid-searched for individual languages on the development data to choose a β value.

Languages that have drastically different performance from the mean warrant closer inspection with confusion matrices. We hypothesize that languages that have multiple very closely related languages in the data set score lower due to frequent confusion with those languages. Alternatively, relatively bad performance can be due to under-representation in the data. Languages that are less common on Twitter run a higher risk of selecting false positives with their key phrases.

Finally, we compare the best greedy selection algorithm with the proposed baseline methods on the test data.

5.1. Phrase Lists

Consider the outcome for English of the 50 phrases based on recall and precision in Figure 2.

As expected, the top 50 phrases selected based on their recall contain stopwords and partial URLs. We find some other interesting Twitter-specific terms such as the hashtag "*#iheartawards*" and chat speak "*lol*", "*twt*" and "*ng*".

Scored by recall rt, https, co, the, to, you, and, my, is, that, for, it, in, of, me, this, no, on, good, are, lol, so, just, your, #iheartawards, can, na, with, what, not, need, too, happy, hahahaha, hello, at, have, from, new, yes, or, thanks, twt, hahaha, ng, how, bye, up, hi, like

Scored by precision to have, of is rt, the we, rt to on, and that, the from, would, their, of on, the rt it, rt is and, the rt at, https to for, when you, the they, being, to who, the your, for on, the as, into, to are, rt she, is on, my with, should, rt see, of in https, https today, rt than, many, rt get co, to our, https his, rt really, my this, for you co, in just, to was, https these, the an, of to https, rt for and, automatically, the up, does, getting, is not, my rt you, it this

Figure 2: Resulting key phrase lists from optimizing on recall, precision and F-score respectively.

The phrases selected by precision instead contain n-grams that combine stop words with partial URLS and less frequent words that are more distinct for English.

5.2. Prevalence effect

Positioned between the precision and recall scoring functions is the selection procedure that weights precision by itself and by recall. By taking an exponentiation of precision we increase its effect in the optimization function, which may be prudent after seeing the non-distinctive selections by recall in the previous section.

The importance of increasing the weight of precision over recall may differ between languages. Instead of looking at any individual language we test three configurations (P^1, P^2 and P^8) on languages binned by their frequency rank from Table 1.

Figure 3 shows that a $\beta > 1$ increases performance for the most common language on Twitter. In the ranks 20-30, however, scoring key phrases on their precision weighted by recall performs best. There are no big differences between values of β. We opt to use $P^2 * R$ for the top 25 languages and $P * R$ for the less common languages in our final scoring function.

5.3. Development Set Performance

Table 2 lists the macro averaged performance for each of the proposed scoring functions. Besides recall we shows *bound recall*, which is the performance of the key phrases under the Twitter rate limit.

Since optimizing recall yields a lot of non-distinctive terms, the retrieved set of tweets proves impure and recall drops when we take the 1% rate limit into account. This is also the case when optimizing precision but respecting a minimum recall threshold of .01.

The three other scoring functions perform better. Simply selecting key phrases on their precision leads to a high precision overall. The yielded 400 high-precision phrases also cover a reasonably large part of the target language tweets (58.67%). The function that selects phrases on the basis

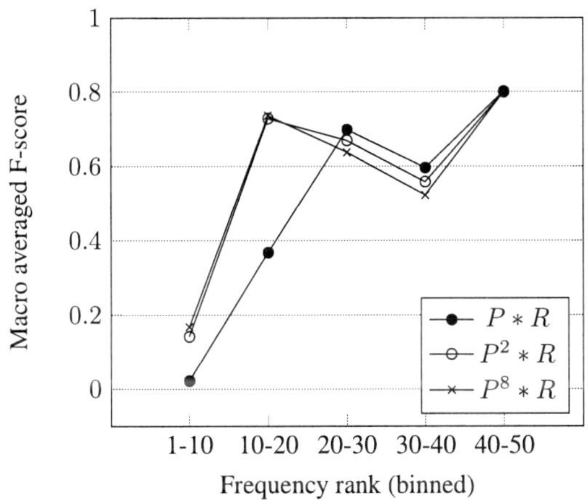

Figure 3: Adding more weight to precision works best for the most prevalent languages on Twitter. Rarer languages benefit from selecting key phrases based on regular precision weighted recall.

Method	Precision	Recall	Bound Recall	F-score
R	16.86%	**85.53%**	1.71%	3.10%
P	**95.17%**	58.76%	45.40%	57.22%
R_p	94.91%	60.85%	45.60%	57.40%
P_r	20.16%	78.93%	2.75%	4.52%
$P^\beta * R$	90.34%	66.24%	**48.37%**	**59.46%**

Table 2: Macro-averaged performance of the different scoring function on the development data. For $P^\beta * R$ we use β of 2 for the 25 most frequent languages in our experiment and β of 1 for the rest.

of their precision but only considers those with a precision higher than 90% performs comparably.
The best overall strategy is scoring phrases on their precision weighted recall with a variable β. Most importantly, this scoring function has the highest recall, even when subject to the Twitter rate limit. We argue that this is usually the objective of collecting Twitter data for a particular target language. For experiments on the test set, we use those lists of key phrases yielded by optimizing in this manner.

5.4. Test Set Performance

Table 3 shows the best greedy algorithm performance on the test set compared to the baselines. Even when selecting the best scoring function on the basis of development set results, it seems that the key phrases performed consistently. There is not big difference between their performance on the development set and the test set.

Method	Precision	Bound Recall	F-score
Baseline 1	14.11%	14.56%	2.64%
Baseline 2	89.58%	40.27%	51.51%
Greedy Selection	**90.38%**	**48.65%**	**59.71%**

Table 3: Performance of the baselines and suggested greedy selection algorithm on the test data.

The macro-averaged scores reported until now are useful in selecting the best general algorithm, but as can be seen in the full results in Appendix Table 6, there is a huge prevalence effect on individual target languages.
Even when accounting for the limit on number of tweets returned at any time, there is some variability in results between individual languages. We look at some of the outliers in detail in the next section.

6. Discussion

Performances for each of the target languages are recorded in Appendix Table 6, and show that while mostly consistent, some outlier results make it harder to discuss findings in a general way.
We mentioned the prevalence effect on recall earlier and thus focus on results that were unexpected with regards to language with similar frequencies on Twitter, specifically Chinese (zh), Esperanto (eo), Galician (gl) and Azerbaijani (az).

6.1. Confusion matrices

Table 4 shows the binary confusion matrices for four outlier results with the three most confused languages. Closer inspection of the confused tweets and selected key phrases give insight into two types of error.
First, for Chinese (zh), tokenization turned out to be a problem. We adopted the Twitter standard from (Twitter, 2019b), which is less suitable for logographic or abjad writing systems. For Japanese, Thai, Korean, Arabac and Hewbrew this turned out not to affect results in any noticeable way. Chinese gets confused often for these other languages however, and only a small portion of the target tweets is retrieved.
Esperanto (eo), Galician (gl) and Azerbaijani (az) all cope with another type of error. Their closeness to a more prevalent language (Spanish for Galician, Turkish for Azerbaijani and multiple highly frequent languages for Esperanto) forces the precision component in the greedy algorithm to select very rare occurrences. Although these phrases are successful in distinguishing between the target and their competition, their infrequency leads to a low recall for the target language in the test set.

	zh	other
ar	2,321	30,517
zh	1,673	3,321
ja	1,010	91,453
ko	228	25,088

(a) Chinese (zh)

	eo	other
eo	423	4,574
en	38	1,8M
es	22	426K
tr	13	81,219

(b) Esperanto (eo)

	gl	other
gl	2,016	2,961
es	1,268	753K
pt	633	453K
fr	102	161K

(c) Galician (gl)

	az	other
az	1,694	3,292
tr	36	583K
en	8	14M
fa	3	90,787

(d) Azerbaijani (az)

Table 4: Confusion matrices for target languages with subpar performances compared to other language with similar prevalence on Twitter.

For each of these outlier cases that bring down averaged performance, it would be interesting to see follow-up research that investigates how much improvement can be made, or whether the problem is with the data and possible code switching that occurs. Framing language identification on Twitter as a single-label problem introduces these inherent pitfalls.

6.2. Robustness and reproducibility

Although there are no major performance differences between applying the key phrase lists to the development and the test split of the data, there could be additional testing on the temporal nature of the lists. Training, development and tests were all performed on data yielded from the same six month snapshot, and could reflect specific events or topics of that period.

For example, the optimized key phrase lists contained 9 hashtags on average. Since hashtags are used mostly as topical and event markers, in a few years these search terms may have disappeared from Twitter completely.

Although this should lead to only marginally lower quality of the supplied phrases, it would be interesting to see an evaluation on data from another period. For now, the robustness of the method for selecting optimal key phrases is not under discussion. The code for generating key phrases on new Twitter snapshots and potentially new target languages is available at `https://github.com/tjkreutz/twitterphrases`.

7. Conclusion

We introduced a systemic way of selecting optimal key phrases for the the 50 most prevalent languages of Twitter. By demonstrating which tweets can be retrieved using the key phrases in an experimental setting that closely mirrors the setup with the real-time Twitter data stream, we provide the statistics that can be cited as limitations for Twitter collections built this way.

The best performing greedy algorithm for selecting key phrases, scores each phrase by precision weighted by recall. For the 25 most prevalent languages, exponentiating the precision with a β of 2 helps to increase the weight of high-precision phrases which limits the number of false positives in the resulting Twitter collection.

Alongside this paper and the code to generate new phrase lists, we provide all the lists as resources. Tracking Norwegian (no) tweets can be as simple as authenticating with your an API key and running curl:

```
    curl -d '@no.txt'
https://stream.twitter.com/1.1/statuses/filter.json
```

The resulting stream should consist of mostly Norwegian ($\pm$96%) language and make up more than half ($\pm$52%) of all available Norwegian tweets.

8. Bibliographical References

Barbaresi, A. (2016). Collection and indexing of tweets with a geographical focus. In *Proceedings of the 4th Workshop on Challenges in the Management of Large Corpora*, CMLC 2016, pages 24–27.

Barnaghi, P., Ghaffari, P., and Breslin, J. G. (2016). Opinion mining and sentiment polarity on twitter and correlation between events and sentiment. In *2016 IEEE Second International Conference on Big Data Computing Service and Applications (BigDataService)*, pages 52–57. IEEE.

Basile, V. and Nissim, M. (2013). Sentiment analysis on italian tweets. In *Proceedings of the 4th Workshop on Computational Approaches to Subjectivity, Sentiment and Social Media Analysis*, SSA 2013, pages 100–107.

Bergsma, S., McNamee, P., Bagdouri, M., Fink, C., and Wilson, T. (2012). Language identification for creating language-specific twitter collections. In *Proceedings of the second workshop on language in social media*, LSM 2012, pages 65–74. Association for Computational Linguistics.

Bloomberg. (2019). How twitter became ubiquitous in japan. `https://www.bloomberg.com/news/articles/2019-05-16/how-twitter-became-ubiquitous-in-japan`. Accessed: 2019-10-21.

Choudhary, N., Singh, R., Rao, V. A., and Shrivastava, M. (2018). Twitter corpus of resource-scarce languages for sentiment analysis and multilingual emoji prediction. In *Proceedings of the 27th International Conference on Computational Linguistics*, COLING 2018, pages 1570–1577.

Eisenstein, J., O'Connor, B., Smith, N. A., and Xing, E. P. (2010). A latent variable model for geographic lexical variation. In *Proceedings of the 2010 Conference on Empirical Methods in Natural Language Processing*, EMNLP '10, pages 1277–1287.

Feige, U. (1998). A threshold of ln n for approximating set cover. *Journal of the ACM (JACM)*, 45(4):634–652.

Grave, E. (2017). Language identification. `https://fasttext.cc/blog/2017/10/02/blog-post.html`. Accessed: 2019-04-24.

Hong, L., Convertino, G., and Chi, E. H. (2011). Language matters in twitter: A large scale study. In *Fifth international AAAI conference on weblogs and social media*.

Huang, Y., Guo, D., Kasakoff, A., and Grieve, J. (2016). Understanding u.s. regional linguistic variation with twitter data analysis. *Computers, Environment and Urban Systems*, 59:244–255.

Joulin, A., Grave, E., Bojanowski, P., and Mikolov, T. (2017). Bag of tricks for efficient text classification. In *Proceedings of the 15th Conference of the European Chapter of the Association for Computational Linguistics: Volume 2, Short Papers*, pages 427–431.

Kreutz, T. and Daelemans, W. (2019). How to optimize your twitter collection. *Computational Linguistics in the Netherlands Journal*, 9:55–66.

Laitinen, M., Lundberg, J., Levin, M., and Martins, R. (2018). The nordic tweet stream: A dynamic real-time monitor corpus of big and rich language data. In *Digital Humanities in the Nordic Countries 3rd Conference*, DHN2018, pages 349–362.

Leetaru, K., Wang, S., Cao, G., Padmanabhan, A., and

Shook, E. (2013). Mapping the global twitter heartbeat: The geography of twitter. *First Monday*, 18(5).

Petrović, S., Osborne, M., and Lavrenko, V. (2010). The edinburgh twitter corpus. In *Proceedings of the NAACL HLT 2010 Workshop on Computational Linguistics in a World of Social Media*, pages 25–26.

Praet, S., Daelemans, W., Kreutz, T., Van Aelst, P., Walgrave, S., and Martens, D. (2018). Issue communication by political parties on twitter. In *Data Science, Journalism & Media 2018, August 20, 2018, London, UK*, pages 1–8.

Scheffler, T. (2014). A german twitter snapshot. In *Proceedings of the Ninth International Conference on Language Resources and Evaluation*, LREC '14, pages 2284–2289.

Semiocast. (2011). Arabic highest growth on twitter english expression stabilizes below 40 `https://semiocast.com/publications/2011_11_24_Arabic_highest_growth_on_Twitter`. Accessed: 2019-10-12.

Tjong Kim Sang, E. and Van den Bosch, A. (2013). Dealing with big data: The case of twitter. *Computational Linguistics in the Netherlands Journal*, 3:121–134.

Twitter. (2019a). Developer agreement and policy. `https://developer.twitter.com/en/developer-terms/agreement-and-policy.html`. Accessed: 2019-06-20.

Twitter. (2019b). Filter realtime tweets. `https://developer.twitter.com/en/docs/tweets/filter-realtime/api-reference/post-statuses-filter.html`. Accessed: 2019-06-25.

Twitter. (2019c). Standard search api. `https://developer.twitter.com/en/docs/tweets/search/api-reference/get-search-tweets.html`. Accessed: 2019-06-25.

Language	ISO	FREQ	MEAN	MAX
English	en	39.06%	39.21%	46.93%
Japanese	ja	19.18%	19.09%	29.64%
Spanish	es	9.52%	9.45%	13.27%
Arabic	ar	7.29%	7.39%	10.82%
Portuguese	pt	5.17%	5.10%	9.59%
Korean	ko	4.43%	4.40%	6.78%
Thai	th	3.61%	3.58%	5.19%
Turkish	tr	2.05%	2.06%	4.04%
French	fr	1.88%	1.88%	3.55%
Chinese	zh	0.92%	0.94%	1.40%
German	de	0.88%	0.88%	1.14%
Indonesian	id	0.88%	0.88%	1.29%
Russian	ru	0.77%	0.78%	1.12%
Italian	it	0.61%	0.61%	0.96%
Telugu	tl	0.40%	0.40%	0.72%
Catalan	ca	0.39%	0.39%	0.68%
Hindi	hi	0.34%	0.34%	0.61%
Polish	pl	0.28%	0.28%	0.47%
Dutch	nl	0.26%	0.26%	0.38%
Persian	fa	0.22%	0.23%	0.42%
Malaysian	ms	0.16%	0.16%	0.23%
Egyptian Ar.	arz	0.15%	0.15%	0.28%
Urdu	ur	0.12%	0.12%	0.20%
Greek	el	0.12%	0.12%	0.20%
Esperanto	eo	0.10%	0.10%	0.10%
Finnish	fi	0.10%	0.10%	0.11%
Swedish	sv	0.09%	0.10%	0.14%
Bulgarian	bg	0.08%	0.07%	0.01%
Tamil	ta	0.07%	0.07%	0.13%
Ukrainian	uk	0.07%	0.07%	0.09%
Hungarian	hu	0.06%	0.06%	0.07%
Serbian	sr	0.06%	0.06%	0.09%
Galician	gl	0.05%	0.05%	0.08%
Cebuano	ceb	0.05%	0.05%	0.07%
Czech	cs	0.04%	0.04%	0.06%
Vietnamese	vi	0.03%	0.03%	0.05%
Kurdish	ckb	0.03%	0.03%	0.06%
Norwegian	no	0.03%	0.03%	0.03%
Danish	da	0.02%	0.02%	0.03%
Romanian	ro	0.02%	0.02%	0.03%
Hebrew	he	0.02%	0.02%	0.03%
Nepali	ne	0.02%	0.02%	0.03%
Bengali	bn	0.01%	0.01%	0.02%
Macedonian	mk	0.01%	0.01%	0.02%
Mongolian	mn	0.01%	0.01%	0.02%
Azerbaijani	az	0.01%	0.01%	0.02%
Marathi	mr	0.01%	0.01%	0.02%
Gujarati	gu	0.01%	0.01%	0.02%
Albanian	sq	0.01%	0.01%	0.01%
Kannada	kn	0.01%	0.01%	0.01%

Table 5: Language frequency (FREQ), averaged frequency per hour (MEAN) and maximum average frequency per hour (MAX) for the 50 languages in our data set.

Language	ISO	Precision	Bound Recall	F-score
English	en	40.21%	1.81%	3.46%
Japanese	ja	65.82%	2.96%	5.66%
Spanish	es	24.40%	2.18%	4.01%
Arabic	ar	80.03%	6.07%	11.28%
Portuguese	pt	89.36%	8.80%	16.03%
Korean	ko	97.73%	10.95%	19.70%
Thai	th	86.80%	11.20%	19.83%
Turkish	tr	94.64%	20.13%	33.19%
French	fr	95.65%	22.28%	36.15%
Chinese	zh	29.98%	3.64%	6.50%
German	de	91.44%	34.05%	49.62%
Indonesian	id	94.51%	39.04%	55.25%
Russian	ru	99.26%	56.17%	71.74%
Italian	it	93.75%	48.48%	63.91%
Telugu	tl	96.84%	81.02%	88.23%
Catalan	ca	97.74%	68.35%	80.44%
Hindi	hi	99.63%	97.86%	98.74%
Polish	pl	98.87%	59.60%	74.37%
Dutch	nl	98.25%	66.12%	79.04%
Persian	fa	99.36%	59.14%	74.15%
Malaysian	ms	93.45%	58.05%	71.62%
Egyptian Ar.	arz	99.78%	54.77%	70.73%
Urdu	ur	99.54%	87.52%	93.15%
Greek	el	99.69%	82.69%	90.39%
Esperanto	eo	81.03%	8.47%	15.33%
Finnish	fi	92.08%	27.70%	42.59%
Swedish	sv	97.42%	63.76%	77.07%
Bulgarian	bg	94.47%	72.51%	82.04%
Tamil	ta	99.80%	79.79%	88.68%
Ukranian	uk	94.62%	44.33%	60.38%
Hungarian	hu	88.78%	25.06%	39.09%
Serbian	sr	93.14%	58.11%	71.57%
Galician	gl	49.28%	8.67%	14.75%
Cebuano	ceb	89.63%	57.10%	69.76%
Czech	cs	98.06%	43.64%	60.40%
Vietnamese	vi	96.06%	76.45%	85.14%
Kurdish	ckb	99.51%	36.72%	53.64%
Norwegian	no	96.05%	51.92%	67.41%
Danish	da	97.14%	56.03%	71.07%
Romanian	ro	95.59%	52.53%	67.80%
Hebrew	he	99.95%	77.91%	87.56%
Nepali	ne	99.32%	88.09%	93.37%
Bengali	bn	99.94%	69.82%	82.21%
Macedonian	mk	99.01%	62.42%	76.57%
Mongolian	mn	99.83%	81.35%	89.65%
Azerbaijani	az	96.97%	33.98%	50.32%
Marathi	mr	97.87%	68.31%	80.46%
Gujarati	gu	99.60%	80.15%	88.82%
Albanian	sq	98.18%	64.01%	77.50%
Kannada	kn	98.72%	60.61%	75.11%

Table 6: Test set performance of individual target languages. In general less prevalent languages are easier to retrieve near-completely.

Association for Computational Linguistics
209 N. Eighth Street
Stroudsburg, Pennsylvania 18360

ISBN 978-1-7138-1251-7
9 781713 812517

CURRAN ASSOCIATES INC.
proceedings.com